Praise for *Difference Making at the Heart of Learning*

A clarion call for helping students build purpose, passions, and how they will contribute into schooling, which is critical if we are to enable all children to fulfill their human potential—and our societal possibilities.

—Michael B. Horn
Co-founder, Clayton Christensen Institute for Disruptive Innovation
Author, *Choosing College* and *Blended*

Vander Ark and Liebtag prove that the future of learning already is with us. It just happens to be scattered. Read this compelling and inspiring account of how "difference making and learning" is at the heart of human purpose, and ask yourself what you can do in your own community to make learning have new and deep meaning. There has never been a time where our combined effort to change the fundamental of learning is so urgently needed.

—Michael Fullan
Professor Emeritus, OISE/University of Toronto

Difference Making at the Heart of Learning beautifully illustrates an educational vision that is simply common sense: If we want to improve the world, we must put that mission at the heart of the learning experience. When students are getting smart to do good for others, they care more, they work harder, and they become better human beings. This book shares inspiring examples from schools and systems all over the world that connect academic learning to civic contribution and the development of ethical character. What could be more important?

—Ron Berger
Chief Academic Officer, EL Education

In a time crisis, Vander Ark and Liebtag's latest book poses an urgent question: "What if learning experiences were focused on making a difference in the world?" The book profiles more than 50 schools where students seek to find the difference they want to make and acquire the skills and knowledge they need along the way. Much more than a powerful call to action, this book represents a turning point in how we think about the purpose of education.

—Tony Wagner
Best-selling author, *The Global Achievement Gap* and *Creating Innovators*

Education is on a journey of transformation and for the past decade Tom Vander Ark and Emily Liebtag have been two of the very best guides. In their new book, they offer "creating difference makers" as a meaningful vision for the future of education and in doing so not only provide a valuable road map but also a powerful destination.

—Ken Kay, Co-founder, P21 and Edleader21
Co-author, *The Leaders Guide to 21st Century Education* and
Bold Moves for 21st Century Leaders

From global pandemics to income inequality, the world faces unprecedented challenges. Today's students may be ones to find a better way forward—but only if they develop their potential as problem solvers and changemakers. In this book, Tom Vander Ark and Emily Liebtag share a hopeful and timely message about what school can be when the focus shifts from content coverage to leadership, problem-solving, and community connections. Plentiful examples from diverse contexts show young people learning by stepping up, taking action, and making a difference.

—Suzie Boss
Project-based learning advocate
Author, *All Together Now: How to Engage Your Stakeholders in Reimagining School*

We all know that the current way of doing school needs an overhaul. This book provides inspiring examples and a compelling vision to put student contribution at the heart of learning. What a refreshing read!

—Julie H. Stern
Co-founder, Education to Save the World
Author, *Tools for Teaching Conceptual Understanding* and *Visible Learning for Social Studies*

We too often focus solely on the what and hows of school; *Difference Making at the Heart of Learning* speaks to our collective WHY for school and community. It's equal parts inspiration to effect change and an actionable playbook to make a difference. Even reading by myself, I felt connected and bonded; I felt the urgent call to action and I felt surrounded by others feeling the same.

—Grant Knowles, Innovation Coordinator
Hamilton County Schools
Chattanooga, TN

Difference Making
at the Heart of
Learning

Difference Making at the Heart of Learning

Students, Schools, and Communities Alive With Possibility

Tom Vander Ark

Emily Liebtag

Foreword by Larry Rosenstock

FOR INFORMATION:

Corwin
A SAGE Company
2455 Teller Road
Thousand Oaks, California 91320
(800) 233-9936
www.corwin.com

SAGE Publications Ltd.
1 Oliver's Yard
55 City Road
London EC1Y 1SP
United Kingdom

SAGE Publications India Pvt. Ltd.
B 1/I 1 Mohan Cooperative Industrial Area
Mathura Road, New Delhi 110 044
India

SAGE Publications Asia-Pacific Pte. Ltd.
18 Cross Street #10-10/11/12
China Square Central
Singapore 048423

Printed in the United States of America

Library of Congress Cataloging-in-Publication Data

Names: Vander Ark, Tom, 1959- author. | Liebtag, Emily, author.

Title: Difference making at the heart of learning : students, schools, and communities alive with possibility / Tom Vander Ark, Emily Liebtag.

Description: Thousand Oaks, California : Corwin Press, [2021] | Includes bibliographical references.

Identifiers: LCCN 2020030592 | ISBN 9781071814857 (paperback) | ISBN 9781071814840 (epub) | ISBN 9781071814833 (epub) | ISBN 9781071814826 (ebook)

Subjects: LCSH: Learning. | Students—Life skills guides. | Community and school. | Transformative learning.

Classification: LCC LB1060 .V36 2021 | DDC 370.15/23—dc23

LC record available at https://lccn.loc.gov/2020030592

Acquisitions Editor: Ariel Curry
Content Development Editor: Jessica Vidal
Editorial Assistant: Caroline Timmings
Project Editor: Amy Schroller
Copy Editor: Integra
Typesetter: Hurix Digital
Proofreader: Ellen Brink
Indexer: Integra
Cover Designer: Rose Storey
Marketing Manager: Sharon Pendergast

This book is printed on acid-free paper.

SUSTAINABLE
FORESTRY
INITIATIVE

Certified Chain of Custody
Promoting Sustainable Forestry
www.sfiprogram.org
SFI-01268

20 21 22 23 24 10 9 8 7 6 5 4 3 2 1

Contents

Foreword

High Tech High was designed as an equity project—a place where students as diverse as San Diego could pursue their passions through community-connected projects. With a lot of community support, the school opened on an abandoned naval base in 2000.

Now a network of 16 schools and a graduate school, High Tech High schools recognize that growth occurs in the context of community and relationships based on trust, caring, and mutual respect. When students engage in work that matters to them and their community, they develop leadership and problem-solving skills that will be valuable for a lifetime.

For a generation of youth facing pandemics, climate change, and the rise of machine learning, it is difference making that is an animating purpose for learning. As Tom and Emily suggest, it might just be the superpower of the new era. Instead of small problems with correct answers, young people deserve an introduction to the challenges and opportunities of our time. It's time to equip them with the tools to make a difference.

—**Larry Rosenstock**
Founder and CEO, High Tech High
Winner, 2019 WISE Prize for Education

Preface

Every individual matters. Every individual has a role to play.
Every individual makes a difference.

—Jane Goodall

We work in a global economy. We share a changing climate. We live, shop, and play on global platforms. One virus—economic, biologic, or technologic—now infects the globe in weeks. We are living in an influential period, what might be a hinge in history, when things could get better for most of the close to eight billion people and future generations—or get drastically worse.

The rise of artificial intelligence and other emerging technologies will produce unprecedented wealth, broader access to clean energy, reduction in tedious work, and the mitigation of disease. But with the benefits come numerous threats, some directly existential and some socially cancerous like spreading inequity.

The climate crisis and the threats of nuclear war and bioterrorism are exacerbated by the widespread use of and access to smart tools. How we share the opportunities and challenges of this new age will have long-term consequences. Decisions taken in this decade will, to a great extent, set the course for life on Earth for this century and several to come.

We're All in This Together

Our challenges and opportunities are shared. In the first third of this book, we make the case for difference making as a part of education and argue that the global nature of new challenges and opportunities call for a new spirit of mutuality. We note that in pursuing the common good in contributions big and small, we thrive individually and collectively as human beings.

Unfortunately, not everyone feels interconnected and supported. Not everyone has a fair chance at prosperity and vitality. Many families struggle to make ends meet. Many young people enter school each day in survival mode feeling disconnected from their peers, their own bodies, and their communities. Young people today find themselves faced with more trauma, racism, mental health issues, hunger, and homelessness than our current systems can support and struggle to find pathways and opportunities to attain a just and equitable life.

There are different beliefs about success and fairness. Some of those differences are honest and some are oppressive. "We can disagree and still love each other, unless your disagreement is rooted in my oppression and denial of my humanity and right to exist," said James Baldwin (Bee and the Fox, 2019). Not everyone believes we're all in this together—and that is often reinforced by active racism and oppressive systems.

We inherited schools designed to sort and segment, which only adds to this feeling of disconnection. We added more tests to spot gaps, but it often narrowed the focus, objectified learners, and reinforced the notion of school as individual work on small tasks.

Our first work is to connect, to create communities and schools where people feel a sense of belonging. We need to start with young people where they are, what they need, and what they care about. Through community-connected projects, young people connect with their strengths and interests, and they gain a sense that they can make a difference.

Everyone Has a Big Next Step

Everyone can make a difference. We believe that everyone has extraordinary potential to do so, and the expanding opportunities that technology brings can exponentially grow our ability to create solutions for our most pressing challenges. It is up to us to prioritize relationships, meaningful work complemented by smart technologies, and helping to unleash the potential of every individual. Prioritizing these challenges and putting them at the center of schooling could lead to a more just, stable and productive world.

At the heart of this new priority set is helping young people find their purpose so that their work is aligned directly to who they want to be and how they uniquely choose they want to contribute.

Leaders must see purpose and belonging as being essential to learning experiences and their strategies if we want entire communities to be uplifted and to lead the way. Ground up "solutionaries" will make the most long-standing positive difference, not leaders who prioritize a test-score-driven agenda.

The new leadership priorities—including equity, problem-solving, agency, and entrepreneurial mindset—accelerate progress educational ecosystems can make towards making a difference.

Difference Making: Schools Alive with Possibility

If we want all young people to have the space to explore strengths, dream possible futures, and begin making their unique contribution, we need schools that are alive with possibility. The concluding chapters in this book provide a glimpse into incredible places and learning experiences that are alive with possibility.

Students need sustained mentors and relationships that support them in their academic, social, emotional, and physical well-being. If we want to be healed, especially those communities who have been oppressed and systematically left out, we have to create connections and meet students where they are.

Institutions of learning have the opportunity to connect talents, purpose, and opportunities for youth—synthesizing who they are with who they want to ultimately become in their lives and in this world. Building on learners' backgrounds, not dismissing them, ought to be at the heart of their experiences in schools.

Schools that do this work well—schools that provide learners the space to explore their purpose and dreams, support to achieve academic, physical, and emotional health, and that help them to connect their goals with opportunities and meaningful projects—are what we should be striving towards. Schools like this, schools alive with possibility, are emerging in cities and towns across the country and around the world.

Thanks to Difference Makers

Our work has taken us to schools and communities around the world, some who have been focused on difference making for years and others who are just realizing its incredible importance in K–12 schools. Observing and learning from leaders in Africa, educators in Kansas City, and students in Albuquerque, have all led us to this book.

From hundreds of school visits and thousands of conversations with students, parents, preachers, policymakers, and the like—making a difference has emerged as the most important way for us to transform learning experiences for young people and build a better future for all.

We deeply thank the thousands of difference makers we've met who inspired this book and who validated our initial hunches and ever-growing conviction that we need to do things differently to better serve our young people. We encourage and call to action others to step up and lead for our current and future learners, because they all deserve to be changemakers and active agents in crafting a better future.

From Global Dignity, "Our Call to Action"

A life of dignity means you are as valuable and important,

worthy and wanted, as any other human being.

It means, fundamentally, that you matter.

And when you believe you matter, then you know

That your voice matters,

Your relationships matter,

And your actions matter.

You have the confidence to act.

You know you will make a positive impact,

That you will work with others

To transform your community—and the world,

Into one where understanding, compassion and love triumph.

You become a changemaker,

Or what we call a dignity-centered leader.

About the Authors

Tom Vander Ark is an advocate for innovations in learning. As CEO of Getting Smart, he advises schools, districts, networks, foundations, and learning organizations on the path forward. A prolific writer and speaker, Tom is author of *Getting Smart, Smart Cities That Work for Everyone, Smart Parents, Better Together,* and *The Power of Place* and has published thousands of articles and co-authored more than 50 books and white papers. He writes regularly on GettingSmart.com, LinkedIn, and contributes to Forbes.

Previously he served as the first Executive Director of Education for the Bill & Melinda Gates Foundation. Tom served as a public school superintendent in Washington State and has extensive private sector experience. Tom is a board member for Education Board Partners; Director for 4.0 Schools, Digital Learning Institute, Latinx Education Collaborative, Mastery Transcript Consortium, and eduInnovation.

Tom has presented at a variety of national conferences, including SXSWEdu, iNACOL's Blended & Online Learning Symposium, ASU/GSV, National Charter Schools Conference, and AACN Annual Meeting. He has also presented at international conferences including the World Bank, the Digital Education Show Middle East, and Bett Show.

Tom received the Distinguished Achievement Medal and graduated from the Colorado School of Mines. He earned an MBA in finance from the University of Denver and continues his education online. Tom is available for all types of speaking and moderating engagements, such as keynotes, panel discussions, round tables, and workshop sessions. Tom regularly speaks on the future of work and learning, leadership, and purpose-driven work.

Emily Liebtag, EdD, supports communities in their efforts to lead innovation and school change from the ground up. Emily has been a teacher in a Title 1 elementary school, an instructor at the University of Virginia, and most recently was the Vice President of Advocacy at a national education firm. She cofounded the nonprofit Boundless, and has helped lead national projects focused on school transformation. Her work on these projects has ranged from designing strategic plans to creating long-term evaluations to hosting community conversations. She has led over 100 learning trips with educators and community members to see innovative practices in schools across the country.

Introduction

....

The world needs your creativity. Now is the time for you
to make your original contribution.

—Michael Toms (M. Toms & J. W. Toms, 1999)

We've entered a new era where life and work are augmented by smart machines and often dictated by the environmental, political, or economic crisis of the week. In a matter of hours, life can be upended by global disasters and worldwide pandemics. Everyone is facing unprecedented novelty and complexity.

This ever changing world and the innovation economy demand a new level of leadership from individuals—more navigating, more empathy, more decisions, and more demonstrated value. For organizations, it means grappling with new problems and organizing quick design sprints around new opportunities in an attempt to try and keep up with the rapidity of change.

Communities are facing unrelenting waves of issues we've never encountered. They need leadership that practices empathy at scale, thrives on iterative problem-solving, and builds strong support for families facing challenges like dislocation, unemployment, and food insecurity.

Communities need leadership that not only calls attention to the inequities across zip codes but leadership that works to actively dismantle systems that inhibit families from thriving and having a fair chance at a good life.

In this perplexing and promising new era, it is contribution that matters—the willingness and ability to step forward and take action to address these challenges, to deliver value, to make a difference. Contribution requires personal leadership, strength of character, and an entrepreneurial mindset. It's as much about problem finding as it is about problem-solving.

Educational institutions in particular have a new job of cultivating difference makers, not test takers. In an era where pedigree matters less than what you have to show in your portfolio, schools have the new priority of helping youth develop a sense of purpose about their place in the world and to support them in their initial contributions.

While public policy hasn't caught up to the new reality, communities that hold conversations about what's happening and how to prepare for the new economy quickly come to agreements about new priorities and the kinds of experiences that develop the skills and character to contribute.

Those with privilege and resources have particular access and opportunities, and therefore an even bigger obligation to contribute to the common good. The challenge for those with power and privilege is to avoid acting on behalf of historically oppressed communities but rather to enlist and empower them to act.

Difference making is the act of co-creating a better union. Everyone can make a difference. Everyone deserves the right to experience the agency of difference making and to benefit from being part of difference makers.

> Difference making is the act of co-creating a better union.

Our goals are to illustrate the benefits of making a difference for both the actor and the community and to make the case that the culture and practice of difference making is valuable in every community—whether well-resourced or historically disadvantaged.

On Discerning the Future

We've spent 20 years studying the future of learning and five years exploring the rise of artificial intelligence and the implications of what's been called the Fourth Industrial Revolution. Despite this deep dive, we appreciate that no one can predict the future, particularly given the rise in complexity of man-made systems and the unpredictable way they are reacting with each other and the ecology. In four decades of attempting to improve schools, build organizations, and mobilize large-scale change, we've seen and experienced more failure than success.

We've observed as many unintended consequences as we have intended outcomes. Through hundreds of conversations and dozens of convenings, we identified important trends and implications of what we are facing and what is to come. With a sense of humility, we offer observations and recommendations on the path forward for schools and communities.

Our work together has focused on innovation for equity. Because we are most concerned about improving historically underserved communities, we write about making a difference and working with purpose with a sense of caution. We attempted to write a book applicable to all communities, particularly historically under-resourced and underserved. We have seen what happens when progress is made for some groups but neglect to pay attention to others. We remain cautious about schools that heed this advice and inadvertently disadvantage young people in some fashion.

We appreciate the benefits of private enterprise and the role it has played in lifting a billion people out of dire poverty in the last 50 years, but we believe accelerating income inequality is as big an existential threat as climate change. Civic and economic systems, particularly in America, have evolved in ways that advantage very large companies and the extremely wealthy. We view the combined rise of climate degradation, income inequality, and nationalistic populism as disastrous for our children and the planet.

It's never been easier for young people to make a difference—to use smart tools to address complex problems—and it's never been more important.

As technology optimists, we appreciate the opportunity of invention, particularly using artificial intelligence, to solve many of the world's most vexing problems. It is our fervent hope that schools will adopt this sense of possibility. It's never been easier for young people to make a difference—to use smart tools to address complex problems—and it's never been more important.

While optimistic about the opportunity, we are concerned about how these benefits of invention will be shared. In fact, the opportunity to contribute may actually be greater in developing solutions that share benefits amongst communities than in the original innovations. As a result, the stories shared in this book are as often about translational innovation and advocacy campaigns as they are about direct solutions.

We entered this 5-year study politically independent but decidedly progressive—socially and educationally. Our concern about economic displacement, accelerating inequality, and climate change deepen our convictions about building a just and sustainable society. Our conclusions about the skills and dispositions required for contribution reinforce what are likely to be considered progressive prescriptions.

Using This Book

One of those unintended consequences we've observed is that the "reforms" enacted on elementary and secondary education systems, particularly in American systems, in the last three decades have locked down a set of structures, routines, and practices that are unproductive, even counter to the kinds of cultures and experiences that young people need to learn to thrive in this new era.

This book calls for big changes in secondary and postsecondary schools—new goals and approaches, new roles for educators, new connections, partners, and policies. It may not be the full blueprint for revolution, but it does lay out a direction with many examples of how our communities can proactively create opportunity for everyone to contribute.

Examples included in this book highlight a diverse range of projects, people and places. We avoid making evaluative judgments on the relative value of individual contributions. We believe the experience and growth of those in service can be even more helpful than the community benefit—especially for young people. No matter how big or how small, people empowered to contribute make an impact on the world.

This book is divided into three parts, each with three chapters:

I. We're All in This Together

II. Everyone Has a Big Next Step

III. Difference Making: Schools Alive With Possibility

Part I of this book provides background on the current realities and opportunities we face as a global society. The first chapter outlines our new mutuality. The second makes the case for difference making. The third chapter introduces the Earth Owner's Manual, the 25 most important issues of our time.

Part II describes how everyone can make a difference. It makes the case for a new set of learning priorities focused on leadership and problem-solving. Chapter 5 describes the benefits of contributing with purpose and how it can ultimately lead to world-changing leaders and ideas. More than ever young people need to feel as if they are working toward finding their purpose in life and contributing in meaningful ways. Chapter 6 describes how community organizations can support difference making.

Part III details how difference making can, and should, be the purpose of learning. Chapter 7 is a brief recap of the history of elementary and secondary education and preview of institutions.

Inventing the future. Chapter 8 highlights schools that put contribution at their core. Schools around the world are alive with possibility. Chapter 9 illustrates how universities are putting difference making at the core. Part III illustrates that anyone can orient their learning toward doing good in the world and that every institution should put difference making at the core.

PART **ONE**

We're All in This Together

It really boils down to this: that all life is interrelated. We are all caught in an inescapable network of mutuality, tied into a single garment of destiny. Whatever affects one directly, affects all indirectly. We are made to live together because of the interrelated structure of reality.

—*Martin Luther King Jr. (Wilson, 2018)*

On Christmas Eve 1967 in his last sermon at Ebenezer Baptist Church, King spoke of the interconnected world in which we live. A half a century later, his prophetic words take on new meaning as we face extraordinary opportunities and existential threats.

The first part of this chapter outlines our new mutuality and responsibility to try and live more interconnected lives. A new mutuality requires more than ever that we depend on and rely on one another. We make the case for making a difference and living in a way that is not just in service of self but that puts the well-being and vitality of others and our communities at the heart of learning and life.

We present an Earth Owners Manual, or the 25 most important issues of our time. We believe these issues ought to be the frame for learning in schools—driving students' lifelong quest to find purpose and contribute through meaningful projects and work.

A New Mutuality

*Change will not come if we wait for some other person or some other time.
We are the ones we've been waiting for. We are the change that we seek.*

—Barack Obama

In 1980, there were no cell phones, laptops, no email, no GPS, no Wikipedia, no search engines, no social media. From a legal pad to a tablet, from drafting board to computer-aided design, from eight-track tape to streaming audio, the 40-year information age transformed the work of almost every sector.

The election of 2016 signaled the end of the information age and the beginning of the automation age. If Barack Obama was elected by social media, Donald Trump was elected by algorithms that exploited social media. By 2016, many of us lived in information gullies co-constructed by bias and bots. Ironically, major-party candidates fought a 1990s battle while the rise of artificial intelligence (AI) became apparent in every aspect of life and work.

In this chapter, we discuss

- The automation economy powered by the Fourth Industrial Revolution
- Three great challenges of economic dislocation and concentration, emerging ethical issues and curbing misuse, and complexity and unpredictability
- Why this time is the best opportunity for difference making we've ever had

The World Economic Forum calls this the Fourth Industrial Revolution. The first industrial revolution, powered by steam, launched mass production. The second revolution added electricity to everything. The third revolution, the information age, added computing power. This new revolution, powered by AI, is adding cognitive capabilities to everything—and it's a game changer.

The concept of AI was conceptualized more than 60 years ago, but the idea that machines could learn from big data sets was so computationally intensive, it was largely dormant for decades. About 10 years ago, computer chips got fast enough that machines could plow through big data sets quickly. In 2011, IBM's Watson, a natural language processing (NLP) system, beat Ken Jennings at Jeopardy, a signal that things were about to change. In 2012, the author (Tom) hosted the Automated Scoring Assessment Prize, which demonstrated that NLP systems could score long and short essays with accuracy matching trained graders.

By mid-decade, neural networks, another category of machine learning, improved dramatically. In 2016, Google's AlphaGo won four of five games in a Go match with champion Lee Sedol. In 2017, language translation systems improved significantly, and Facebook added facial recognition.

Simultaneous with the rapid development of machine intelligence was the explosion of the internet of things (IoT)—billions of connected sensors in everything and cameras everywhere. Applications include home and commercial security, medical monitoring, transportation and logistics. There are more than 20 billion connected devices worldwide and could be more than 50 billion by the end of the decade (Statista, 2019). All of these phones, sensors, and cameras produce mountains of data that feed machine learning algorithms used in every sector of the economy.

The third part of the automation age revolution (with AI and IoT) is the enabling technologies that produce tangible benefits: automated manufacturing systems, robots, delivery drones, autonomous vehicles, drug discovery systems, and gene editing tools. The combination of machines that learn from sensors everywhere and convert intelligence into benefits offers unparalleled opportunity for contributions to health, longevity, safety, and prosperity.

Great benefits and unprecedented wealth are being created by this revolution, but it comes with three great challenges. The first is economic dislocation and concentration of benefit. The second is new ethical issues and emerging forms of misuse. The third is the complexification of how human systems interact with one another and the planet.

Dislocation and Concentration

AI, particularly machine learning, and related exponential technologies are quickly augmenting many tasks at home and work. They will increasingly displace jobs while creating new entrepreneurial opportunities. There are many competing claims about how severe the displacement will be and to what extent it will be offset by new jobs. It appears clear that displacement will vary by sector and geography, but it will be significant and it will begin before today's middle school students graduate and join the workforce. It is also clear that more people will be out of work more frequently with repeated, even continuous need for upskilling (upgrading their skills in new arenas).

Compared to prior revolutions, this one is occurring at an exponential speed. Some predict that we will see more change in the next 20 years than we have in the last 300 years (Leonhard, 2016). While impacts may be ubiquitous, control is unusually concentrated. AI is a centralizing force—it plows through monster data sets in seconds, aggregating benefits and wealth at an unprecedented speed. It propelled tech giants Apple, Amazon, Microsoft, and Google to market valuations of more than one trillion dollars (at least before the pandemic crash) and produced many of the 2,100 billionaires on the planet (again, pre-crash). Two dozen billionaires have the combined wealth of the poorest half of the world's population (Oxfam, 2019).

Code that learns is both powerful and dangerous. It threatens the basic rules of markets and civic life. It's curating almost every screen you read, exacerbating racial bias through things like facial recognition for policing and making or influencing decisions about hiring, loans, and jail sentences.

AI is reshaping life and livelihoods. And without forward-looking civic leaders and quick and thoughtful action, the wealth and benefits will be highly concentrated, leading to conflict and more reactionary politics.

AI requires a new technical and civic infrastructure, a new way to conduct business, a new way to be together in community. Needless to say, the technology is moving faster than new social agreements. The potent combination of technologies is swamping communities with complex issues and a combination of predictable and unanticipated consequences.

Technology Through a Lens of Equity and Social Justice

Washington Leadership Academy (WLA) opened in the nation's capital in 2016 after winning an XQ Superschool grant. Its mission is "to prepare our kids to thrive in the world and change it for the better."

All WLA students take 4 years of computer science and coding. WLA students—almost all of whom are people of color and from low-income households—look at technology through a lens of equity and social justice. They study the intersection of technology and public policy; listen to guest speakers, often also people of color who work in the tech sector; and learn how tech can strengthen their communities.

In other words, they don't just learn how to operate computers. They learn how computers influence society.

"The way we teach computer science is not strictly about coding, because coding always changes," said Jordan Budisantoso, one of WLA's five computer science teachers. "It's about how to think about problems. It's about logic. It's about gaining an understanding of how technology shapes our world" (XQ Institute, 2019, December 9).

All WLA students participate in internships with government, private sector, or nonprofit organizations during the eleventh grade.

Curbing the Misuse of Smart Machines

Code that learns is aiding every aspect of life. We can look forward to more convenience, less disease, cleaner energy, and safer and cheaper transportation. But AI is moving faster than public policy. In addition to job dislocation and growing inequality, there are opportunities in three areas to shape the future for good and curb misuse of AI: discrimination, autonomous weapons, and excessive surveillance.

Discrimination

As more machines make more judgments, we're seeing old biases baked into decisions about facial recognition, criminal sentencing, and mortgage approval.

"Algorithmic bias is shaping up to be a major societal issue at a critical moment in the evolution of machine learning and AI," said the MIT Tech Review (Knight, 2017). "If the bias lurking inside the algorithms that make ever-more-important decisions goes unrecognized and unchecked, it could have serious negative consequences, especially for poorer communities and minorities."

"Because math is involved people think it leaves out bias, but it's only operating on the data from humans," said Olin professor Amon Millner (T. Vander Ark, 2019, March 20), stressing that if the data are inequitable, bias will be present in the recommendations for who gets a job, who gets a loan, and who goes to jail.

"We need diverse teams to study how we're applying algorithms to ensure that we treat people fairly," said Millner (T. Vander Ark, 2019, March 20). He's worried that right now these decisions are being made by teams that are not very diverse in race and gender.

The more insipid self-imposed threat of discrimination is our own media feed trained by a series of selections and swipes that over time create a filter bubble that narrows the scope of content to which we are exposed.

Exploring the Ethics of Artificial Intelligence in Middle School

In the fall of 2017, Justin Aglio spotted AI as a game-changing trend. The Director of Academic Achievement and District Innovation at Montour School District created partnerships with nearby Carnegie Mellon University and with MIT to "develop a program in artificial intelligence (AI), providing students with a myriad of opportunities to explore and experience AI, using it to cultivate, nurture, and enhance initiatives aimed at increasing the public good (2018)."

In 2018, the district launched a middle school ethics course developed with MIT Media Lab to explore the ethical issues AI presents and to study how ethical AI could be created. Case studies explored algorithmic bias and fairness, facial recognition, and privacy.

Why start in middle school? Blakeley Payne from the Media Lab notes that, on average, children receive a cell phone around age 10 and open a social media account when they are 12 (Aglio, 2019). Their screen time is being curated by AI.

In addition to ethics, Montour middle schoolers dive into autonomous robotics and make AI music. Montour teachers embedded AI units into Media Arts, STEM, Music, and Computer Science classes.

"The goal for the program is to make an all-inclusive AI program for all middle school students that is relevant and meaningful in a world where children live and prepare them for a future where they will thrive," said Aglio.

Killer Robots

Team MAVLAB from Delft University of Technology won the $1 million first prize in the 2019 AI Robotic Racing Circuit race. Lockheed Martin sponsored the competition to showcase drone capabilities and catalyze innovation in autonomous systems command and control.

While drones promise inexpensive fast delivery and affordable monitoring in many sectors, the flip side is that drones are being weaponized and are changing the character of warfare as evidenced by the flock of Iranian drones and missiles that crippled a Saudi oil refinery in September 2019. The attack made clear that a fleet of cheap drones poses a threat to individual targets as well as big targets like ships and bases. With more autonomy, these weapons will pose an even greater threat.

The Campaign to Stop Killer Robots was formed in 2012 to counter the threat of machines gone bad. The campaign, backed by Tesla's Elon Musk and Alphabet's Mustafa Suleyman, seeks to ban such machines outright. The United Nations is also scrambling to get ahead of this threat. As chair of the United Nations' Convention on Conventional Weapons, Amandeep Gill has the difficult task of leading 125 member states through discussions on the thorny technical and ethical issue of killer robots.

Surveillance

Chinese municipalities are using facial recognition technology and AI to clamp down on crime. The Chinese Ministry of Public Security said that in 2020 they will have 626 million cameras in an unprecedented national surveillance system (Keegan, 2019). Beijing-based SenseTime, the world's most valuable AI company, claimed in 2018 that Guangzhou's public security bureau had identified more than 2,000 crime suspects with the help of the technology.

China is also rolling out a social credit system that tracks the activities of citizens to rank them with scores that can determine whether they can be barred from accessing everything from plane flights to certain online dating services (Kobie, 2019).

A majority of hedge funds are now using AI and machine learning to help them make trades. This has all made markets faster, more efficient, and more accessible to online investors. However, a Bloomberg reporter said, "The kinds of data that the really high-end firms are using isn't as anonymized as you might think." And for some investors, "there's a lot of information about you that can be traced to you specifically" (Wood, 2019).

The explosion of cameras and sensors and expanding use of AI is boosting the amount and type of information being tracked about every person, making it possible to link data and make inferences about each of us. College students are being surveilled as they walk across campus and enter lecture halls (NPR, 2019). These emerging capabilities represent unimagined difference-making opportunities and substantial, even existential, risks.

Take Waze, a popular transportation app, which started as a GPS and mapping tool, is curtailing traffic and guiding our driving behaviors with predictive analytics and countless data points being collected by the second. Waze isn't just a map app anymore; it is influencing our driving behaviors and beliefs about communities.

AI is currently smart in narrow bands, but the next few decades will, given the drive of curiosity and profit, bring about broader forms of intelligence, what some call Artificial General Intelligence. The risk, says Berkeley's Stuart Russell, is less the malice of science fiction movies, but rather more the competence of smart machines to accomplish goals that are not well aligned with ours (Russell, 2019). Managing AI alignment may prove to be humankind's most important accomplishment—or our biggest failure.

The difference—likely to be a hinge in history where things get better for most people or worse—is likely to be whether AI is approached with a contribution or extraction mindset. If investors and developers seek to exploit short-term opportunities for personal gain, AI will increasingly be a threat to the public good. But if policymakers, users, and funders and developers embrace a contribution mindset—with a focus on doing the most good for the most people in the long run—there is a good chance that our children will experience the benefits of health and prosperity.

New and Different Challenges

The Fourth Industrial Revolution is racing around a planet ravaged by the first three. We are probably six decades into the Anthropocene, a new geologic era where the byproducts of human activity have altered the climate and landscape of the planet (Turney et al., 2018). The result is a predictably less predictable climate system.

With terrible force, the summer of 2017 brought a series of once-in-a-century storms that swamped the southern United States. In December 2017, the Thomas Fire burned more than a quarter million acres in Ventura and Santa Barbara Counties—only to be nearly doubled in devastation 11 months later by the Mendocino and Camp fires. The November 2018 California wildfires brought even more devastation, making them the most expensive in history (Gee, 2019).

After the California wildfires, the most expensive disaster of 2019 was Typhoon Hagibis, which caused about $15 billion damage in Japan. "Storms like Hagibis are growing more common, and at a surprising pace," Said science writer Erick Mack (Forbes, 2019).

Early 2020 brought the COVID-19 pandemic worldwide, bringing much of the global economy to a standstill and halting many services, education, and public gatherings and causing hundreds of thousands of deaths.

These unanticipated and unprecedented events are suggestive of a new era where evolving natural systems collide with complex human systems in unpredictable ways, an era of novelty and complexity. We are not yet equipped as a species to handle the complexities we have created.

The New Mutuality

The rise of AI will produce unprecedented wealth, broader access to clean energy, and the mitigation of disease and drudgery. But with the benefits of AI come numerous threats—some directly existential and some socially cancerous, like spreading inequity. Sharing the benefits and taking action to mitigate the risks require a new sense of mutuality.

The climate crisis is one big collective action problem. We need to stop taking carbon out of the ground and putting it into the atmosphere. We need to find ways to take carbon out of the atmosphere and put it in the ground. The former will throw millions out of work and we'll need to find ways to support their transition. The latter will take public investment and support for entrepreneurship. We need to reduce consumption and increase invention—it's a collective action problem.

It is increasingly one climate system, one economy, and one media market. In a growing number of ways, small and large, we are all connected. We are all in this together.

No Better Time to Make a Difference

What does this all mean for teaching and learning? What does it mean for communities seeking to improve their educational ecosystems? How do these new technologies impact our livelihood and economy? It means it is time we come together to rethink how we interact, engage, and design for novelty and complexity. This new era undoubtedly yields paradoxical implications, but it also presents incredible opportunities to create a better future for all.

The good news first: It has never been easier to make a difference—and the opportunity set improves every month. Many of the world's great challenges and opportunities will be addressed by teams equipped with smart tools. The potential to curtail disease, create clean energy, automate manual tasks, expand access to abundance lifestyles, and explore the universe is imminent and exciting. It's never been easier for young people to learn, connect, launch an impact campaign, code an application, or start a business.

The flip side is that current challenges, particularly climate change and unsustainable inequity, require immediate and global action. The wealthiest people in the world—like Jeff Bezos, who committed $10 billion to fight climate change—are taking the initiative in their own hands if world leaders are choosing not to. Each month, new technology adds puzzling ethical questions and compounds existential threats. The one thing we can be sure of is that we—and especially our children—will see more rapid and complex change than ever before. From this, we conclude that Seth Godin's 2012 insight was spot on—that our educational priorities should be leadership and solving interesting problems (Schawbel, 2014).

In Chapter 2, we summarize how, given our current realities and unforeseeable future, we have to double down on creating meaning and purpose in school, work, and lives of young people. We detail the benefits of leading with contribution and how it not only makes a difference in communities but in our overall mental health and well-being.

CHAPTER
TWO

We Thrive by Contributing

The purpose of life is to discover your gift.
The work of life is to develop it.
The meaning of life is to give your gift away.

—*David Viscott (1993)*

The shock of the November 2016 presidential election activated student Liam Neupert: "I felt devastated and absolutely terrified of what was to come in the next four years" (Anderson-Minshall, 2019).

Fortunately, the gay biracial Boise teenager had a good friend to talk to; "It is so crucial for everyone to have someone or something that allows them to take the time and search through their feelings."

Neupert also had supportive parents and a new school in Boise that helped him channel his concern into action. He began advocating for LGBTQ rights in the Idaho legislature and volunteered with a peer-led sex education class where teens learn a comprehensive approach to sexual health and teach it to other teens.

In March 2019, as a junior at One Stone, Neupert led the Idaho climate strike that brought hundreds of young people to the capitol steps. About his school community, Neupert said, "We constantly advocate for what we believe in. We have created a community around this problem; we have created a very large ripple effect."

"The big thing I've really seen open up in my life during my time at One Stone is my mindfulness . . . I've grown in a way where I am mindfully focusing more on how I am consuming and impacting our planet."

The vegan fashion trendsetter also reduced his consumption of fast fashion brands after looking at the carbon footprint and employment practices of leading brands. He began to shop second-hand and look for brands that are transparent about their practices.

Neupert, who has become a regional leader on environmental issues, said, "School should be about exploring your passion—authentically you—as well as things you're not always engaged in."

Neupert serves on the board of the school that is raising an "army of good for good." The 2019 cohort of One Stone students in the Lab School and after-school program completed over 400 projects, many of which were in service to the community, including parent and teen discussions about alcohol abuse; teaching middle school girls about healthy relationships and behaviors; a campaign to reduce waste from single-use cups; a campaign to fight drinking and driving on graduation night; taking refugees on outdoor adventures, and three-dimensional printing parts for local businesses (T. Vander Ark, 2019, October 21).

The project topics are student generated or generated by the community. Both students and coaches are informed by community input. At the beginning of the school year, One Stone issued a "Request for Problems" to its local partners that would be used to inform their investigations and contributions.

"Students are willing and ready to talk about tough topics that adults are often conditioned to steer away from," explained founder Teresa Poppen. At One Stone, they don't shy away from difficult subjects like depression and substance abuse. When they host community conversations, adults are often surprised at the poised and thoughtful ways One Stone students address emerging issues.

In this chapter, we discuss

- Contribution as not a new idea but a way of being in community that dates back to the earliest years of our existence as a species
- How leading with making a difference might be the way to change the world and that there is no better time to make a difference than now
- The psychological, mental, and physical benefits of leading with contribution
- How contribution builds community and connects us to the ever growing social economy

One Stone is one of the growing number of school communities dedicated to equip and empower youth to contribute to the common good. The idea is new to modern public education, but it has been central to all of the great faith traditions and foundational to civilizations that flourish.

Contribution Is Ancient Wisdom

As long as people have been living in community, there has been an ethic of mutualism and a practical wisdom of purposeful service. Spurred by a mix of mindfulness, gratitude, and obligation, all of the great faith traditions which built global communities value contribution.

The Jewish tradition of *Tikkun Olam* involves acts of kindness to perfect or repair the world. It implies that each person has a hand in working toward the betterment of his or her own existence, as well as the lives of future generations—it asks people to take ownership of their world (Noparstak, n.d.).

Repair the World by Repairing Lives

Kim Lathrop was born with no arms or legs. She lives on her own and every day is a challenge. A team of Bay Area makers created a device that helps Kim grab things with her mouth and bring them closer for ease of use. The simple device is inexpensive to produce and could improve the lives of paraplegics worldwide.

The maker community that addressed Kim's need is a chapter of Tikkun Olam Makers (TOM), a global movement that "creates and disseminates affordable solutions to neglected challenges of people living with disabilities, the elderly and the poor."

TOM teams identify neglected challenges, prototype affordable solutions, upgrade what works into products, and disseminate solutions to end-users. Three dozen global TOM communities are supported by Reut, an Israeli social impact group founded by Gidi Grinstein in 2004.

We find this emphasis on contribution in other faith traditions as well. For example, Father of the Protestant Reformation, Martin Luther, viewed vocation as the locus of the Christian life. He said the purpose of every vocation is to love and serve your neighbors. God does not need your good works, Luther said, but your neighbor does (Veith, 2016). Social welfare is a principal value in the Islamic tradition. The practice of service to humanity is widely instructed and encouraged (Stefon, 2010). The high holy days of Passover, Easter, and Ramadan all celebrate reconciliation. The world's great religions teach this spirit of making all things new in daily life.

Working for Social Justice and Human Dignity in Chicago

Billy Moore did 20 years of hard time for a murder he committed as a young man. For more than a decade after his release, he has worked as a life coach for other ex-cons for The Inner-City Muslim Action Network (IMAN), a community organization that fosters health, wellness and healing in the inner-city by organizing for social change, cultivating the arts, and operating a holistic health center.

The IMAN vision is "To serve as the model of the Muslim tradition of facilitating transformational change in urban communities, by inspiring others towards critical civic engagement exemplifying prophetic compassion in the work for social justice and human dignity beyond the barriers of religion, ethnicity, and nationality."

The nonprofit was formed in 1997 by Dr. Rami Nashashibi and is guided by deep spiritual convictions around principles of human dignity, social justice, and compassion, particularly for marginalized people of color in the inner city.

Dana, acts of generosity and giving, is the first theme in Buddhism. A kind and compassionate attitude toward every living being and the world is central to Buddhist teaching (Moffitt, n.d.). And the indigenous approach to living sustainably is based on nurturing relationships in communities through sharing and the understanding that our planet is a living entity that must be cared for and preserved for future generations (Share the World's Resources, 2010).

Teaching Civic Virtues

The new reality is that many young people do not grow up in communities of practiced religion. Generation Z is the least religious generation. Instead, "Post-Millennials live in a culture of choice, self-actualization and freedom of expression," said Sacred Heart Professor Christel Manning (2019).

While positive for a sense of tolerance and opportunity seeking, this trend of non-religiosity raises questions. Will more young people grow up outside communities of caring adults? How will young people be exposed to role models of contribution?

Contributing to the common good is a civic virtue. It's one of four elements of practical wisdom identified by the Jubilee Centre for Character and Virtue at the University of Birmingham. The others are intellectual virtues like curiosity and critical thinking, moral virtues including compassion and integrity, and performance values of getting work done with persistence and collaboration.

Developing these virtues—what some might call character education—has been a historical component of schooling, from ancient through modern times, with the exception of a few decades at the end of the 20th century in many Western democracies.

After more than two decades of preoccupation with grade-level testing in reading and math, a growing number of schools in the United States and around the world are returning to broader aims, with contribution at the core.

And rather than reading about character in a textbook, more schools are taking an applied approach and supporting youth-led efforts to serve the community. Finding a way to make a difference in the community uniquely develops all the top skills—self-direction, curiosity, and civic identity—identified by Turnaround for Children's Building Blocks for Learning, a framework for the development of skills children need for success in school and beyond (Stafford-Brizard & Cantor, 2016).

The Building Blocks report makes clear that these priority skills are built through modeling, support, and opportunities to apply and transfer them independently. Relationships and social context are keys.

"Empowering All Students to Make Meaningful Contributions to the World"

That is the remarkable motto of the Loudoun County Public Schools, a sprawling district northwest of Washington, DC, serving about 84,000 students in 94 schools.

In his 5 years as superintendent in Loudoun, Dr. Eric Williams led community conversations that resulted in updating district aims. While many districts reference citizenship as a goal, Williams appreciates the personal nature of contribution and the breadth of expression in private sector careers, community service, and civic engagement.

He believes in "engaging students in solving authentic problems as a means to developing students as knowledgeable critical thinkers, communicators, collaborators, creators, and contributors."

"When learners see themselves as an entrepreneur now, when there is a real audience for their work now, they have a strong sense of ownership of their work," said Williams

In elementary school, Williams looks for students working in small groups to solve an authentic problem. They might consult an expert to develop a knowledge base and then share the solution with that expert.

At one Loudoun middle school, several students struggled with cancer. Their classmates developed projects to learn about different types of cancer and raise funds for a cure. "We want to see learners choosing a problem and coming up with solutions across content areas," said Williams.

Another elementary school developed pitches for Amazon's second headquarters. Students did a ton of research on local geographic and economic strengths and they developed pitches on why Amazon should locate its second headquarters in Loudoun. Economic development officials and Amazon Web Services executives came and listened to the student proposals.

Middle school students developed pitches for historical markers. Based on a student proposal, the state approved a monument at the Ashburn Colored School, which served African American students during the era of segregation.

At a Loudoun high school, students developed a project to test road de-icing materials that were alternatives to traditional, more environmentally damaging de-icers. Students pitched their ideas to community experts, including state transportation officials and promoted the alternative de-icers through social media and homeowner association newsletters.

Williams believes in "engaging students in solving authentic problems as a means to developing as knowledgeable critical thinkers, communicators, collaborators, creators, and contributors."

"Having students focus on authentic problems can be a game-changer," added Williams. "Ownership leads to persistence. Learning will be deeper. Student ownership of their work leads to persistence when the work becomes difficult. And ultimately learning will be deeper and longer lasting" ("Eric Williams" 2019).

What If Impacting the World Was the Goal?

Educators working with high school students observe a good deal of boredom. They often ask about how to engage students so that they learn the required content. Sasha Barab (an Arizona State professor) thinks that is the wrong question (Peters, 2019).

Barab suggests a thought experiment: What would happen if educators reversed the core assumptions, beginning with the interrelations of person, content, and context and then put emphasis on how to leverage success with particulars to generate appreciation of universals?

In other words, what if we started with the learner and what they care about?

"In contrast," argues Barab, "when one treats impacting the world as the goal, then the criteria for success becomes whether the individual can, and chooses to, leverage the to-be-learned content in ways that are relevant to goals that they view as important."

"In this redesign," explains Barab, "the focus is on learners making progress in situations that they care about and for which universals have value." In contrast to systems that privilege only content, a redesign would put person and context on equal footing.

"Such a system would prioritize people thriving in particular situations, not on consuming content in ways that might have value in some future situation."

Imagine schools that were laboratories of transformation—of people and communities—rather than places where formulas and facts were memorized. Imagine if schools helped young people to understand who they are, what they're good at, and where they will make their initial contribution.

Barab concludes,

> By starting with the specific use cases that learners care about and the progress they wish to make in these situations, or even that the educators wanted them to make, one would begin to see the power of the situation and the learner, resulting in an educational system that valued making awesome people who can do great things over one that primarily cares about disembodied articulations.

EL Education Focuses on Contribution

EL Education is a national network of schools and a leading curriculum provider with a three-dimensional vision of achievement where students master knowledge and skills, develop character, and create high-quality work.

At the heart of character is the ideal of contributing to a better world—students "putting their learning to use as active citizens, working for social justice, environmental stewardship, and healthy, equitable communities (e.g., citizenship, service, advocacy)."

The character core is supported by helping learners develop a positive identity. That includes agency, purpose, and belonging. The academic environment is designed to support character growth through compelling curriculum, student-engaged assessment, deeper instruction, and a student advisory called Crew.

A middle school example of students contributing to a better world is Polaris Charter Academy in Chicago where 96% of students knew a gunshot victim. Students met with community stakeholders, researched peacekeepers, wrote a book, created public service announcements, and organized a citywide day of peace (EL Education, n.d.)

Benefit Mindset in Leadership

A new priority for school leaders might be to develop a benefit mindset, one that is focused on doing good and not just personal gain. Developing a benefit mindset pushes beyond development and gain purely for individual growth and puts others, well-being and development into the equation. School leaders who look past supporting individuals getting ahead at the expense of others and optimize the opportunities for collective growth and good embrace this mindset.

Ashley Buchanan, Director at Cohere, describes it as building on a growth mindset and "not only [where we] seek to fulfil our potential, but choose to do it in a way that serves the wellbeing of all" (Benefit Mindset, n.d.). The Benefit Mindset School Guide invites educators to consider a new way of thinking about the purpose of learning and to consider contribution as a central priority of learning.

Buchanan and Kern (2017) write:

> The Benefit Mindset describes everyday leaders who discover their strengths to make valuable contributions to causes that are greater than the self, leaders who believe in

"Everyone deserves an education that is about their own development as a human being," said Peter Senge. "The purpose of education—is for me to become me—in the context of the society that I live, so I can truly contribute to my society" (TaishiConsulting10, 2012).

If impacting the world was the purpose of education and a focal point for schools, the potential to change the world and to uplift communities is endless. Not only is it a key to our future, but difference making is motivating, supported by science, and easier than ever.

Difference Making Is Motivating

Speaking to better preparation and motivation, Google's Jaime Casap frequently says, "Don't ask a student what she wants to be when she grows up. Ask her what problem she wants to solve" (T. Vander Ark, 2017, January 24).

Focusing on local versions of global problems and opportunities makes learning authentic, integrated, and community connected. Young people

Exploring Real-World Problems

Del Lago Academy—Campus of Applied Science is a public high school in Escondido, just north of San Diego. It's a single pathway school focused on health and biotechnology.

Del Lago scholars are challenged to explore real-world problems that extend beyond the classroom by establishing side-by-side working relationships with industry mentors.

"We believe students who are challenged intellectually by actively exploring real-world problems value their learning and are motivated to succeed," said principal Ruth Hellams (2019).

The mission includes preparing "innovators who create solutions to local and global problems through empathy, creativity, and collaboration."

Another mission component is to create "world citizens who are respectful, responsible, ethical, and compassionate." This aspiration is addressed, in part, through the advisory system, a weekly opportunity for scholars to meet and share their awareness and appreciation of others' culture, values, and diversity. They build stronger relationships with each other and enhance community and well-being.

Student tour guides at De Lago gladly explain the five pillars that serve as mutual agreements of how they live and work together: Welcome, Do No Harm, Never Too Late To Learn, Choice Words, Be The Best.

Robert, a senior, found "Be the Best" to be motivating. He knew all the faculty and took advantage of the fact that they all care. After experiencing success at Del Lago in digital media, virtual reality, and podcasting, Robert is heading to UCLA film school.

gain confidence as they experience success and contribute to their communities. Students are more motivated by real-world tasks and learning that has purpose. True projects and learning that is focused on making a difference is innately real world and authentic (Lombardi, 2007).

Difference making can fuel a greater motivation for learning communication skills that otherwise might have seemed less interesting to develop or taking on a bigger problem than the learner thought they could possibly handle. When a learner knows they are going to impact a real person, place, or challenge, it drives deeper learning.

Michael Joyner was an indifferent high school student in Tucson. After graduating, he tried several colleges before ending up at the University of Arizona where he joined the track team but almost flunked out. He decided he'd become a fireman and signed up for the test. Because he was a runner, a graduate student asked Joyner if he wanted to be a subject in a study on lactic acid. He showed up and ran in the lab, and told Freakonomics, "Man, this is unbelievable. There's actually people who do this for a living" (Dubner, 2020).

The head of the physiology lab told Joyner he could be a student assistant if he got his grades up. He started getting straight As. "I saw that if you wanted to do studies in humans where you put catheters in and do biopsies and that sort of thing, it would be facilitated if you were a physician," explained Joyner. He went to medical school to become a research physiologist. Today, Dr. Joyner is a professor at the Mayo Clinic and is what Freakonomics (2019) called "a big deal in the field of exercise physiology."

Joyner's story illustrates the power of purpose and how quickly a bad student can become an academic star when there is a clear path to contribution. His accidental appearance in the lab that turned into a productive career is also a reminder of how important broad exposure, work experiences, and good guidance are to helping young people connect with a sense of purpose.

"If you are motivated, you learn better and remember more of what you learned" (Murayama, 2018). The science of motivation points us to contribution and difference making time and time again, including in Joyner's case. Whether motivated by rewards, intrinsic or extrinsic, or by the change and chemistry in the brain when one makes a connection to another human, we all can benefit from making a difference.

Increased academic motivation can not only come from seeing yourself on a path to contribution but by helping others. High school students raise their own academic achievement by giving advice to younger students on how to improve study habits, upending traditional beliefs about how to boost motivation and performance for struggling students.

"When someone is struggling to meet their goals, we intuitively believe that giving them advice may improve their performance," said Wharton researcher Lauren Eskreis-Winkler. A Character Lab study revealed that the inverse was true: "We increase individual motivation and ultimately performance by placing students in a position to give, rather than receive, help. If we want to motivate kids, we should give them opportunities to help others" (Eskreis-Winkler, Milkman, Gromet, & Duckworth, 2019).

The Psychology Behind Making a Difference

Young people are now more likely to choose a job based on how it enables them to contribute to something larger than themselves (Peters, 2019). This is supported by several global surveys, including a 2019 Deloitte survey of over 60% of millennials who shared that a sense of purpose is why they work for the company (Peters, 2019). Another 2016 survey of millennials showed that more than 64% of employees would consider a company's social and environmental commitments when deciding whether it was a place they wanted to work (Cone Communications, 2016).

Our future (and likely a large portion of our current) workforce wants to have jobs where they are making a difference (Deloitte, 2019). Many millennials surveyed said they wanted to work for a company that was focused on "improving society rather than just generating profits" (Fink, 2019).

Companies like Patagonia have declared that they are in the business of making a difference in the world and that they want employees who are dedicated to doing good in the world.

Certified B Corporations, including Patagonia, are businesses that meet high standards of verified social and environmental performance, public transparency, and legal accountability to balance profit and purpose. The growing number of so-called B Corps are accelerating a shift to redefine success in business and build a more inclusive and sustainable economy. B Corps use profits and growth as a means to a greater end: positive impact for their employees, communities, and the environment. The B Corp community works toward reduced inequality and poverty, a healthier environment, stronger communities, and more high-quality jobs with dignity and purpose. Nonprofit B Lab certifies company claims and annually honors top changemakers for their impact on the world (B Corps, 2019).

This growing preference for purposeful work—in jobs and in school—is not just psychological, it is biological. Numerous studies reveal that there are also cognitive impacts when we engage in difference making. Endorphins are released when we provide help to others and there are other neurological benefits to engaging in acts of service (Haupt, 2010; Luks & Payne, 2001; Rusu, 2019).

Dr. Patricia Boyle, a neuropsychologist focused on studying Alzheimer's Disease, shared that "working toward a goal and feeling like you are making a contribution to society likely increases your sense of purpose in life, which we have found contributes to both psychological and physical health" (Rush, n.d.).

Finding your purpose and finding work aligned to this purpose have also been found to have positive effects on our overall well-being. Khullar, physician at New York-Presbyterian Hospital and a researcher at the Weill Cornell Department of Healthcare Policy and Research, writes, "Research increasingly suggests that purpose is important for a meaningful life—but also for a healthy life. Purpose and meaning are connected to . . . well-being." Khullar (2018) continues and shares several positive health benefits of having a purpose, including lower risk of dementia, better sleep and fewer strokes and heart attacks.

In schools, where many students psychologically are struggling due to trauma, biological needs, or other challenges they face, providing them space to find their purpose and enhance their well-being makes sense. A study of 10th graders who randomly were assigned to volunteer weekly showed that after 4 months they had lower levels of inflammation, better cholesterol profiles, and lower body mass index. Students who had the biggest increases in levels of empathy and altruism also had the largest reductions in cardiovascular health risk (Schreier, Schonert-Reichl, & Chen, 2013).

Difference Making Is Easier Than Ever

In August 2018, Swedish activist Greta Thunberg sat outside Sweden's Parliament holding a simple sign that said "School Strike for Climate." Just over a year later, she had four million social media followers, had mobilized 13 million climate strikers in 30 countries, and was *Time's* Person of the Year.

It was free social media, short-form video, and digital infrastructure for memberships and event planning that helped Thunberg activate leaders like One Stone student Liam Nuepert worldwide. Similarly, the shooting survivors from Marjory Stoneman Douglas High School (featured in Chapter 3) vaulted to national prominence after organizing highly visible gun control events. Both gun control and climate change groups would say they haven't achieved their desired impact yet, but they have changed the national perception—and much faster and more efficiently than was ever possible.

Communication applications like WhatsApp and WeChat make it easier for initiative organizers to communicate nationally and globally. Open tools on sites like Code.org make it easier to learn to code an impact application. AWS Educate makes it fast and free to learn cloud computing technology. It's getting easier to access open source machine learning tools like TensorFlow from Google, PyTorch from Facebook, and Azure from Microsoft. GitHub provides the code needed to power world-class software.

A growing number of commerce platforms make it easier to launch a business: marketplaces like eBay and Etsy; commerce platforms including Shopify, Squarespace, and Weebly; and backed supports like Fulfillment by Amazon. Influencers make real money on YouTube and Instagram.

It's increasingly easy to raise money for a good cause. About $250 billion in venture capital flowed to startups in 2019—about half internationally. Twice that amount was invested philanthropically in the United States alone.

One illustration of smart money flowing to good ideas is the Emerson Collective, an initiative of Lauren Powell Jobs to transform health, education, media, and spread social justice. In venture capital, Village Capital supports impact-driven, seed-stage startups worldwide. Since 2009, they have worked with more than 1,100 entrepreneurs in 28 countries and invested in 110 startups.

Chole Capital is funding female-led startups taking on big challenges like climate change and nutrition. Whoever you are, wherever you are, it is easier to gain access to the right kind of capital—grants, loans, or impact focused equity—for difference making.

These innovations have also made the path to difference faster than ever. The ability to take an emerging idea, share it with the world, get feedback, find followers who support you, and then reach the world all within 24 hours is an unprecedented opportunity more young people ought to be taking advantage of.

The Coming Social Economy

"Humans generally find their place in life through contribution," said Jeff Fray, psychologist and Senior Vice President at the growth platform Gloo, "and it is this desire to contribute that is the massively latent human resource that will drive tomorrow's social economy" (T. Vander Ark, 2019, April 11).

Gig work platforms will continue to surface more opportunities to contribute. Enabled by more participation and outcome data, it will become easier to value contributions in ways beyond clocking time. Measures of delivered value could include the traits that make us uniquely human—care, consideration, creativity, and critical thinking.

"Measured efficacy will unlock the new social economy," said Fray. "Data will tell the value creation story of how well one person supports the growth of another."

As populations age and as automation eats rule-based jobs, the need and opportunity for the social economy will expand. The social economy will be built on the traits that make us uniquely human—care, compassion, creativity, and critical thinking.

These types of contributions will eventually supersede the weight of an applicant's test scores or their ability to follow a script. Quality of interactions, meaningful relationships, and commitment to a cause will reign as more valuable, both in schools and in the workplace.

"Humans generally find their place in life through contribution," said Jeff Fray, psychologist and SVP at the growth platform Gloo, "and it is this desire to contribute that is the massively latent human resource that will drive tomorrow's social economy."

Grappling With Global Issues at IDEA

Innovation, Design, Entrepreneurship Academy (IDEA) is a small high school in Dallas focused on social entrepreneurship. Students use design thinking to attack Global Goals for Sustainable Development, identify an area of passion, and learn about how they can make a difference.

IDEA has a strong commitment to learning through internships and mentorship. It has an advisory meeting every morning. Students are supported in choosing an internship.

There are no sports at IDEA, but students lead interest-based clubs for academics.

IDEA operates as a community. There are regular "family meetings" of restorative practices that are student led and support learners in developing conflict resolution skills.

Students appreciate working at their pace and for having personalized options as well as flexible space in the school for learning. One student shared, "Personalized learning is working at your own pace, in a way you can be successful" (Midles, 2019).

The goal is to prepare young innovators to launch an impact-driven business before they graduate.

Unfortunately, many communities still struggle to gain adequate access to networks, connections, and resources that make this opportunity to make a difference so ripe. Struggling to connect or having a quality device to connect with shouldn't be a barrier in 2020, but for many it is.

Contribution Builds Communities

Melinda Gates is a leader who has committed her life to making a difference and to creating more access and opportunities for others. Her impetus for dedicating her life to this work might in part be driven by how motivating it is, but it is far more likely that uplifting communities is her driving cause.

She writes in her book *The Moment of Lift: How Empowering Women Changes the World*, "How can we summon a moment of lift for human beings—and especially for women? Because when you lift women up, you lift up humanity" (Gates, 2019, p. 2). She is committed to lifting up the voices and stories, particularly those of women, who are helping their communities around the world.

Like Gates, we have been fortunate and excited to see cities and communities around the world uplifting, gaining hope and viability as a result of individual schools or educational ecosystems choosing to make a difference.

A shift to making a difference in schools doesn't only benefit the students directly; it also can uplift entire communities and groups of people.

Contribution is the innovation economy superpower. By taking on a complicated local problem and delivering value to a community, young people build agency and practice design thinking. It's why Seth Godin frequently says that young people should learn to lead and solve interesting problems.

In places like the rural town of Kearney, Missouri, students are working on projects that benefit their town and local economies. Former Superintendent Bill Nicely wanted to see Kearney be a place to stay and live, not just a place to "get out of." Kearney has been ranked as one of the fastest growing cities in Missouri.

Marion is a small town north of Columbus, Ohio, with a history of manufacturing. When Gary Barber took over as superintendent in Marion in 2012, he listened to the community. He recognized that relational partnerships are critical to community improvement. He formed a design team that included the chamber of commerce, local colleges, and economic development partners. Together they developed new learning goals, including "A Marion City graduate will be responsibly engaged in the community, take initiative and show empathy, be experienced in the community and in leadership roles." They experienced a resurgence as a result of shifting high school priorities to focus on providing more meaning and relevance to high schoolers. New program Global Logistics Pathway leveraged local opportunities and partnerships (Vandeborne & Fujii, 2016). The district, as of spring 2020, has a new design team that is refreshing the portrait of a graduate.

Communities like Pittsburgh are being reinvigorated by efforts like Remake Learning, a festival of innovative learning practices and contribution of ideas making a difference in the lives of youth in the city. Scott Peck, as quoted by hooks (2018, p. 52), shares: "In and through community is the salvation of the world" (Peck, 1998).

The benefits of contributing to the common good are embedded in wisdom traditions and should be central to education. Not only does it benefit the community, but it's a shortcut to building the most important skills for life.

Ironically, the best preparation for a future full of novelty and complexity is helping young people make a contribution here and now. Rather than focus on what kids might need 15 years in the future, engaging young people in complex problem-solving and delivering value builds agency, collaboration, and subject matter expertise.

Earth Owner's Manual

Not only is it the case that happy people are more willing to help others, but as I generally point out, helping others is the best way to help yourself, the best way to promote your own happiness. It is you, yourself, who will receive the benefit.

—Dalai Lama

During a philosophy degree at Oxford, Will MacAskill decided to give away a good portion of what he made as a researcher. With doctoral student Toby Ord, MacAskill formed nonprofit Giving What We Can in 2009. In the first year, dozens of people joined them and pledged $21 million.

After his degree, MacAskill and Oxford colleague Benjamin Todd were trying to figure out what to do. They laid out a set of principles and a process to figure out where they could make a difference. It turned into a lecture, a student organization, then a full-blown organization dedicated to how to best use a career to make a difference. They figured you have about 80,000 working hours in your career (40 years × 50 weeks × 40 hours), so they called the project 80,000 Hours.

In this chapter, we discuss

- How this generation will face unprecedented challenges and opportunities
- How effective altruists maximize the impact of their careers
- The 25 most important issues of our time that could frame learning

They developed a guidance framework with the Future of Humanity Institute for those seeking to make a difference. It suggests working on big problems that are highly neglected but solvable.

For people seeking to use their careers to make a difference, they developed a set of postulates:

- **Impartial concern for welfare:** give equal weight to everyone's interests. Avoid privileging the interests of others based on arbitrary factors such as their race, gender, or nationality. Consider the impact on future generations.

- **Effective altruism.** The top priority in doing good is to get the big picture right and not to sweat the details. If you can do better on the big decisions, then you can have hundreds of times more impact than what's typical.

- **Expected value and counterfactuals.** Expect the unexpected when trying to do good. Consider all of the good and bad things that could result from our actions, and weigh them by the probability that they will actually happen.

- **Longtermism.** To consider the full consequences of our actions, we must consider potential effects on future generations.

- **Moral uncertainty and moderation.** Focus on increasing long-term welfare, uphold cooperative norms and factor in a variety of reasonable ethical perspectives.

With blogs, podcasts, and a job board, the 80,000 Hours organization aims to help people maximize their positive impact on the greater good in their professional lives. They advise picking issues where additional resources will have the greatest returns.

With some sense of priority, you can test personal fit: where do you have the highest chances of excelling? Does it fit with the rest of your life and risk tolerance? Will it let you contribute to a pressing problem right away?

Driving Questions

Effective altruists like MacAskill focus on making the biggest difference they can by focusing their research and teaching to helping others find the most valuable ways to spend their careers. He got there by asking big questions. Education, on the other hand, asks young people small procedural questions in narrow categories of knowledge called disciplines.

With few if any immersive experiences and big integrated projects, high school students and college freshman and sophomores have little chance to dive into the biggest questions. They learn small chunks of knowledge, regurgitate it for a test, and frequently don't learn why it's important to them. They don't see possible futures much less have the opportunity to immerse themselves in possible futures for extended periods. We ask small questions with right answers, but young people live in a complicated world with no easy answers. What if we encouraged young people to ask more big questions—the kinds that are important to them and their community but don't have easy answers? Big questions like how might we provide access to justice for all? Or how might we create livable and workable cities?

Wrestling with big questions obviously requires learning some building blocks of knowledge, but it can be done with purpose and motivation.

The 200 project-based schools in the New Tech Network frame each unit of study with a big driving question. On visits to Katherine Smith Elementary in San Jose, we've seen classrooms take on big questions, including:

- How can we design and evaluate a solution to the over consumption of one of Earth's natural resources?

- How can we promote healthy habits in ourselves and our community?

- How can we create a video game based on ancient Greece?

- Given a budget, how can we design a home for a family while taking into consideration location; space; time, labor, and materials; and personal preferences?

- How can we (as second graders) provide a valuable product to customers?

Possibility Thinking in Pittsburgh

Combine a makerspace, science fair, and a coding bootcamp and you have South Fayette School District, a computational carnival for 3,200 students south of Pittsburgh. With four schools on one suburban campus, South Fayette has integrated computational thinking K–12. Students are learning to code, but more importantly, they are learning to attack complex problems, analyze data, and sprint in teams to public products.

South Fayette integrates its approach to computational thinking with habits of mind of successful problem solvers. That includes dealing with complexity, persistence, and tolerance for ambiguity. It includes human-centered design thinking strategies and visible thinking. Computational thinking is also embedded in career awareness, which includes contexts where the problem-solving processes, dispositions, and attitudes apply. This helps students understand and envision how those careers reflect their learning.

"Our partnership with Carnegie Mellon University is critical in developing robust pathways and ecologies in computer science and engineering at South Fayette, from high school to university and beyond," said Aileen Owens, Director of Technology and Innovation.

Aileen Owens said that developing student agency and leadership has been core to the South Fayette transformation. Students have learned with teachers and even taken on teaching roles.

"Systems thinking is a mindset for innovation," said Owens. She described the iterative process of innovation and of developing small-scale incubations before full-scale implementation.

The sense of possibility starts early in South Fayette. We visited a primary classroom that was exhibiting their smart city model complete with QR codes and online explanations.

Generation Z is the first to experience the impact of dramatic climate change—terrible storms, violent fires, and rising sea levels—and perhaps the last generation with a chance to effect a sustainable change. This is also the first generation to live and work in the era of smart machines. It will be the first to experience superintelligent machines and help communities deal with all of the ethical issues associated with sharing the benefits and guarding against existential risks.

These great forces, climate change and artificial intelligence, are likely to be influential in shaping life on Earth in the coming years, but they represent only two of several dozens of the most important issues of our time. The 17 Sustainable Development Goals (SDGs) adopted by the United Nations (UN) in 2015 are a good start at identifying actions that will make life better, sustainable, and more equitable for more people.

Thousands of teachers around the world have committed to incorporating the Global Goals into their classrooms and advocating for them in their communities to help achieve the goals by 2030. The group, called Teach SDGs, expands in cohorts each year and shares successes on social media (#TeachSDGs).

25 Most Important Issues of Our Time

There are (at least) 25 important issues of our time that create urgency for our current and next generations to be solution-generators. The UN SDGs are a good starting point—a baseline for planetary justice and sustainability. It is, however, problem focused and missing a few emerging issues and impact opportunities. To make the list something like an owner's manual for the planet, we consulted expert organizations that have made similar efforts to enumerate the important issues of our time. They included the Grand

The 25 Most Important Issues in the World

Adopted in 2015 by world leaders, the United Nations Sustainable Development Goals provide a road map to a better future:

1. **No poverty:** End poverty in all its forms everywhere.
2. **Zero hunger:** End hunger, achieve food security and improved nutrition and promote sustainable agriculture.
3. **Good health and well-being:** Ensure healthy lives and promote well-being for all at all ages.
4. **Quality education:** Ensure inclusive and equitable quality education and promote lifelong learning opportunities for all.
5. **Gender equality:** Achieve gender equality and empower all women and girls.
6. **Clean water and sanitation:** Ensure availability and sustainable management of water and sanitation for all.
7. **Affordable and clean energy:** Ensure access to affordable, reliable, sustainable, and modern energy for all.
8. **Decent work and economic growth:** Promote sustained, inclusive, and sustainable economic growth; full and productive employment; and decent work for all.

9. **Industry, innovation, and infrastructure:** Build resilient infrastructure, promote inclusive and sustainable industrialization, and foster innovation.

10. **Reduced inequalities:** Reduce inequality within and among countries.

11. **Sustainable cities and communities:** Make cities and human settlements inclusive, safe, resilient, and sustainable.

12. **Responsible consumption and production:** Ensure sustainable consumption and production patterns.

13. **Climate action:** Take urgent action to combat climate change and its impacts.

14. **Life below water:** Conserve and sustainably use the oceans, seas, and marine resources for sustainable development.

15. **Life on land:** Protect, restore, and promote sustainable use of terrestrial ecosystems, sustainably manage forests, combat desertification, and halt and reverse land degradation and halt biodiversity loss.

16. **Peace, justice, and strong institutions:** Promote peaceful and inclusive societies for sustainable development, provide access to justice for all, and build effective, accountable, and inclusive institutions at all levels.

17. **Partnerships for the goals:** Strengthen the means of implementation and revitalize the global partnership for sustainable development (The Global Goals, n.d.).

    The National Academy for Engineering with support from other leading think tanks adds a few emerging challenges and opportunities (National Academy of Engineering, n.d.)

18. **Understand the brain:** Predict how interactions between the physical and social environment enable behavior. Inform AI and advances in health care, manufacturing, and communication.

19. **Cyber security:** Prevent intentional or unintentional attacks on public systems and uses of AI systems that do harm or pose an existential risk (Future of Humanity Institute, n.d.).

20. **Prevent nuclear terror:** A global war could kill a large percentage of the human population, and the resulting nuclear winter could be even deadlier than the war itself (Future of Life Institute, n.d.b)

21. **Biotechnology for good:** Reduce risk from especially dangerous pathogens and curb negative effects of cloning, gene splicing, and a host of other genetics-related advancements (Future of Humanity Institute, n.d.; Future of Life Institute, n.d.a).

22. **Engineer the tools of scientific discovery:** Acquire new knowledge about the physical and biological worlds; expand access to data science and impact partnerships.

    The last three are widely supported but differently phrased contribution opportunities:

23. **Powerful expressions:** Extending the quality of and access to human expression and visual and performing arts.

24. **Getting along:** Values serve as a pillar of a healthy society (Global Shapers Community, n.d.). They are complemented by empathy, perspective, and self-regulation (Knowledge Works, 2017). They empower difference making in a diverse society (Asia Society, n.d.).

25. **Extraplanetary Life:** Exploration of space and the potential for life on other planets. Jeff Bezos said, "We humans have to go to space if we are going to continue to have a thriving civilization." And, "Eventually it will be much cheaper and simpler to make really complicated things, like microprocessors and everything, in space" (Clifford, 2019).

From *24 Goals to Save the Planet* (T. Vander Ark, 2020)

Challenges for Engineering from the National Academy of Engineering, the Bill & Melinda Gates Foundation Grand Challenges, and the Global Shapers Community sponsored by the World Economic Forum. We also consulted the Future of Life Institute, Future of Humanity Institute, National Science Foundation, and Seth Godin (2018) (who built his own list of 23 problems worth solving).

The list of the most important issues of our time could serve as an Earth Owner's Manual, a guide for difference makers. It could be used as a framework for schools to introduce young people to the issues of our time in a relevant way that allows them to start contributing right now.

How to Get Started

What if, instead of teaching subjects in high school, we allowed students to explore the Global Goals that provide a road map for a just and sustainable future while they learn about their strengths, interests, and values, and where they want to begin making a difference?

If half of high school were devoted to projects exploring the Global Goals (and the other half to skill building), there would be time for a week or two on each goal and three or four deep dives for juniors and seniors. Integrate a few projects, and you've got a great opportunity to teach history and science in the making. Every goal has a big data set behind it, which is well suited for math applications.

If it feels daunting to redesign a high school around the Earth Owner's Manual, teachers can start small and look for opportunities to weave the goals into the curriculum. Pick Martin Luther King Jr. Day, for example, and use it as an opportunity to study the history and future of efforts to reduce inequality (Goal #10) in America. Use the goals to inspire knowledge, skill, and action.

Starting to work on these goals does not have to be a massive undertaking, rather find ways to start small and act locally. While the goals pertain to global issues, there is probably a local version of the problem that learners can address. The community you teach in likely is experiencing a challenge that learners can incorporate into a project or a design challenge.

Integrating subject areas into cross curricular projects can also be a good starting point. Time is of the essence in core subject area classes, often leaving educators feeling as though there is no choice but to teach their standards. But when even two subject areas are taught and there are natural and meaningful ways that learners can apply what they are learning, the engagement and deeper learning increase.

Learners all deserve to know they can make a difference, and K–12 experiences ought to provide them opportunities to see themselves as being able to make positive change in their communities. No matter how big or how small, if it is locally or globally; everyone has a big next step.

PART **TWO**

Everyone Has a Big Next Step

One child, one teacher, one book, one pen can change the world.

—Malala

Everyone has extraordinary potential to make a difference and it has never been easier or more important—it is the new superpower in our ever-changing world and economy.

In Part II, we share new priorities for learning and leading: Learning focused on calling and finding purpose through meaningful work. Leading centered on making a difference in the world and providing educators and learners the greatest potential to do just that.

We also share why purpose and finding your calling really matter. We reveal examples of incredible outcomes communities have seen when educational ecosystems make purpose a top priority. Centuries of wisdom inform us that finding one's true calling and purpose in life is what leads us to meaning and forward progress as a society.

It might be cliche, but it is true—"Whether you think you can or you can't; you're right." We aim to empower all young people to believe that they *can* and provide them with experiences and environments that encourage them to make a difference in the world. Everyone has a big next step and in this section of the book we highlight how to make that happen in schools.

Learning to Lead

The possibility that lies before us, the chance to connect, to lead, to be heard–it's bigger than it's ever been.

—Seth Godin (2020)

After a cheating and corruption scandal, the El Paso Independent School District was taken over by a state-appointed board of managers in 2014. They appointed a nontraditional superintendent, Juan Cabrera. As a former teacher, a school district lawyer, entrepreneur, and technology executive, Cabrera said in his introduction to the community, "Education has been my lifelong passion" (T. Vander Ark, 2016).

Having led big businesses around the world, Cabrera had a pretty good sense of what young people needed to know and be able to do. But rather than incorporating his view into the turnaround plan, his new leadership team held over 50 community, staff, and student input sessions that gathered input from over 2,000 participants. They asked, "What's happening? What does it mean? And, What do we want El Paso students to know and be able to do?"

Consistent themes emerged from these conversations: critical and creative thinkers and problem solvers; responsible leaders and citizens; and bilingual communicators. The resulting El Paso graduate profile (below) changed the priority in the district from a focus on test preparation to active learning with a focus on leading, problem-solving, and informed citizenship.

| Critical knowledgeable and creative thinkers | Informed problem solvers | Effective bilingual communicators | Responsible leaders and productive citizens | Socially and emotionally intelligent individuals |

The El Paso focus on learning to lead and solve problems echoes marketing guru Seth Godin's summary of what's important—learning to lead and solve interesting problems (Godin, 2012). If the El Paso story teaches us anything, it is that new leadership priorities can drastically drive and shift what teaching and learning looks like in educational systems.

In this chapter, we discuss

- The new education priorities are leadership and problem-solving—spotting opportunities, mobilizing a team, and delivering value for a community.
- Difference-making skills and dispositions include equity, agency, effectiveness, inclusion, global citizenship, entrepreneurial mindset, collaboration, and design thinking.
- To develop schools alive with possibility, the new skill priorities are as important for educators as students.

New Priorities

For the last 20 years in America, standardized testing of grade level proficiency in reading and math has been the driving priority in education. Basic skills are obviously important, but the reductive mechanical view of school as test scores has damaged the profession of teaching and dehumanized the process of learning.

In a world where new and different is the norm, where complex systems collide in unexpected ways, where opportunity is sprinting as fast as inequality, it's time for new education priorities. The massive shutdown of schools in the spring of 2020 due to COVID-19 highlighted for millions what is relevant to be learning in schools versus what hasn't been working for so many learners.

It's time for school communities to adopt new priorities relevant to the innovation economy, to help every learner develop the agency to lead and the curiosity and capability to take on high-impact problems. It's time to value the public products of difference making over test scores. It's time to help learners connect with a sense of purpose and build capabilities for difference making.

Simply put, young people need to learn to lead and solve interesting problems. In this chapter, we discuss the eight skills and dispositions that enable difference making: a commitment to equity, leading with inclusion, agency, personal effectiveness, global citizenship, entrepreneurial mindset, collaboration, and design thinking.

These leadership skills and dispositions can be taught explicitly but are best "caught" in a culture that shares them as core values. When schools adopt these new priorities, difference making is the mission, and the needs of the community and interests of students are at the core. Sir Ken Robinson shares in *Finding Your Element* (2014) an important message about difference

New Learning Priorities for Difference Making

LEADERSHIP

PROBLEM-SOLVING

Effectiveness:
self-knowledge and management, good decision making

Agency:
capacity to act on the world

Global Citizenship:
activate global goals with cultural competence

Equity:
Seeing what should not be and envisioning what could be to create a more inclusive world

Entrepreneurial Mindset:
spotting opportunity and delivering impact

Collaboration:
social awareness, relationship skills, enabling others

Design Thinking
Creative problem-solving using a design thinking process

making for leaders: "What you do for yourself dies with you when you leave this world, what you do for others lives on forever."

Equity at the Heart of Leadership

Leadership for difference making starts with a commitment to equity—a recognition of the dignity of each person and working to actively dismantle systems that do not support each person thriving. Equity at the center of leadership means prioritizing student, family, and community needs. These leaders recognize the urgency to change things that need changing. They spot opportunities, they notice when things are not the way they are supposed to be, and they start taking action.

Equity is central to all of the other priorities, as this is where the work should start. Pursuing other priorities without understanding the needs of a community can unknowingly deepen or recreate inequities. Facing the oppressive systems and policies that harm families head-on is nonnegotiable when it comes to designing better educational ecosystems. It is an ongoing priority, not something that can be checked off and completed in a one-time meeting. Ibram Kendi (2017), Professor of International Relations, shares in a speech at Bates College, "The mind is complex, and when we think of any personality trait that we're striving to get away from"—like racism—"it's an everyday process."

Leading for equity means seeing assets and value in a community as well as where there are opportunities and needs. Leaders who are centered on creating more equitable ecosystems make the case for change, enlist the support of others, mobilize change efforts, and iterate solutions until they deliver value to the community. Ignited by a sense of the possibility, leaders begin with humility, include others, contribute generously, and thank frequently.

For educators, the leading for equity question is, "How might we provoke and support student leadership for all learners?" Developing young leaders means giving them opportunities to lead with both formal leadership roles and informal student identified opportunities.

We look to others who do this work well to provide us guidance and support. The National Equity Project, Equity Institute, and The Equity Collaborative provide good starting points for leaders. Schools in the Big Picture Learning network explicitly prioritize equity in their leadership framework. The international network of student-centered schools promote a compulsion toward equity and the moral courage to speak and act against dis-equitable systems and structures.

When leaders, like those in the Big Picture Learning network, prioritize equity, then learners should experience very different environments. For example, learners in project-based New Tech Network schools have the opportunity to lead project teams several times each year.

All students at Katherine Smith School in San Jose (the first New Tech elementary school) have the opportunity to serve as school and classroom ambassadors. While providing informative school tours, ambassadors are building agency, leadership, communication, and project management skills. Even in primary grades, ambassadors are well prepared and confident representatives. After each tour, ambassadors debrief with the principal on successes and growth opportunities.

Where High School Starts With Leadership and Design Thinking

Freshmen at LEAD Innovation Studio learn design thinking and leadership. The third-year high school option is part of the Park Hill School District north of Kansas City.

Maliyah enrolled because she liked the focus on leadership and service. In her freshmen design class, she expressed her concern about the walking safety of her siblings and designed plans for a wireless device that triggers an alarm and sends the location to emergency services. The local police gave her positive feedback which ignited additional work. She applied for and received a provisional patent for the device. As a sophomore, she met with manufacturers and worked on a prototype.

In the leadership class, LEAD learners develop success skills, project management, and impact strategies. They study how nonprofit organizations support the community. Some students volunteer, others launch awareness campaigns.

Students in the Palo Alto High School Journalism program lead 10 publications including a newspaper, public affairs journal, arts and culture journal, and yearbook. Students learn the basics in a 20-week journalism class. Then they have the chance to join a highly respected publication and get published. Most 10th graders show up waiting for someone to tell them what to do. "When they realize that they are in control, it gets exciting," said Wojcicki (2019). "They learn fast, and once they feel confident it spreads to their entire life—a mindset that all students should have."

Power is dispersed as widely as possible among student teams beginning with five editors in chief. "These are regular kids who rise to become amazing," said Wojcicki.

Building Personal Effectiveness

Vera is a sophomore at Crosstown High in Memphis (featured in Chapter 8) where two of the 12 core competencies are developing self-knowledge and leading your own learning. She said teachers trust them to do the work but many "struggle with leading their own learning—it's hard sometimes to stay on task."

Instead of being spoon-fed worksheets, Crosstown students engage in community-connected projects. Vera added, "It forces you to learn more about yourself and learn what's best for me and ask myself what environments do I learn best in."

Managing your attention, your time, and your work is key to success in any endeavor. The skills are more important than ever with more complicated work and more distractions.

Personal effectiveness is three of the five core competencies the leading advocacy organization CASEL calls social and emotional learning. Self-knowledge is the ability to recognize your thoughts and emotions and how they influence behavior. It's the knowledge that capability grows with effort (often called growth mindset). Self-management is regulating emotions and behaviors in different situations and working toward personal and academic goals. Responsible decision-making is making constructive choices about personal actions and interactions. Developing these traits of personal effectiveness requires real work and real responsibility.

Del Lago Academy in the Escondido Union High School District north of San Diego prioritizes competencies that the biotechnology, health care, and local businesses value. Founding Principal Keith Nuthall created an environment where scholars are challenged intellectually by actively exploring real-world problems. At Del Lago, "scholars read, write, think and behave like scientists, mathematicians, historians, and artists." Scholars earn badges for planning and self-direction as well as experimentation and communication through internships and projects.

Developing Agency

Marie Bjerede progressed from engineer to high-tech general manager because she had great technical skills and the ability to communicate and collaborate. Leading Qualcomm's Design Center, she studied human motivation and became an early advocate of self-organizing teams. In attacking adaptive problems, it was creativity and collaboration that mattered. The most successful engineers didn't wait to be told what to do; they understood the goals and took initiative.

It's this sense of agency that Bjerede thinks will be the most important employment skill. It's a confidence that one can affect their future and surroundings. It's the expectation that everyone should be respected (Getting Smart, 2018, January 17).

In the future of work, everybody will constantly need to prove themselves, said Bjerede. We will all face adaptive challenges, new and different from anything we've seen, and agency will be key.

Developing personal agency—the ability to act on the world—starts with volition. Rather than responding to rewards and punishments, peer or parental pressure, Bjerede said young people develop agency in the pursuit of their own goals, and they need opportunities to take action (Bjerede, 2018).

The new economy requires and rewards leadership and it starts with agency—self-awareness of skills and interests and having experienced success in making a difference. Leaders who ask themselves, ". . . not how they can flourish in isolation, but rather, how we can all come together and become partners in each other's flourishing. Our ability to flourish is deeply interrelated with the communities and ecosystems to which we belong" (Buchanan & Kern, 2017, p. 6).

Equipping Community Health Advocates

Imagine a health high school that is not just a talent pipeline for hospitals but an advocacy organization for a healthier community. Imagine a school that asks local providers for input on projects of current community significance.

Health Leadership High School in Albuquerque is a small school for students not well served by traditional schools. The project-based school prepares young people to become community leaders in health care and beyond. Health Leadership is part of a network of cause and career-focused schools in Albuquerque.

"We don't have classes," said Executive Director Blanca López. "We have projects. Most students work on three projects per day. It's the main focus of the school."

Each summer, the staff solicits project ideas from community health providers. Community Engagement Director, Moneka Stevens, leads the effort to engage all the health-care providers in the city to propose projects.

Every project must have deliverables valuable to the community. "We see where needs are. We create advocates for change," added López.

Health Leadership serves about 180 youth aged from 14 years to 24 years. "We want kids to see themselves as leaders in the community," said López.

Director of Curriculum & Instruction Amber Reno explains the link between community-connected projects and student supports. "We ask more than regular schools," said Amber. As a result, the school sees tremendous growth between each of the three student presentations annually (T. Vander Ark, 2018, April 24).

Cultivating Global Citizenship

Difference makers see the big picture. They may be working on a local issue, but they connect it to the global community. This connection ties self, to society, to the greater well-being of all people. Leaders that prioritize this interconnected and dependent relationship between local and global are helping to prepare learners for a global world. Mandela worked hard to support his own country, but he did not do it in hopes that it *only* benefited his people.

The Asia Society is the recognized expert on global competence. It suggests that global competence is developed through knowledge and skill in four areas: investigating the world, recognizing perspectives, communicating ideas, and taking action. "Globally competent students have the skills and knowledge to not just learn about the world, but also to make a difference in the world" (Asia Society, n.d.). Since 2003, The Asia Society has supported two dozen public schools promoting global competence through the International Studies Schools Network.

The opening story about El Paso is an example of a school district committed to supporting a bicultural, biliterate community. Superintendent Cabrera believes dual language programs are not just an equity issue, they're an economic development issue; "We all live in a border economy. Multilingualism should be seen as an asset the way it is seen internationally—and we need that mindset in the United States if we are going to stay globally competitive" (2017).

Entrepreneurial Mindset

"Learning things that matter; learning in context; learning in teams. Envisioning what has never been and doing whatever it takes to make it happen. Do that 20 times and you will be employable forever," said Richard Miller, President of Olin College of Engineering (Vander Ark, 2019, February 25).

Miller started thinking about this formula more than 20 years ago. When the trustees of the F. W. Olin Foundation began contemplating a new approach to engineering education, they formed Olin College and Miller signed on as the first employee. The first faculty members joined in September 2000. And, in a nod to how different Olin would be, they invited 30 students to help design the curriculum. Living in modular buildings, they joined the faculty in studying new approaches to engineering education. A full class was enrolled in 2002.

With about 350 students, Olin is small in size but large in impact. It was recognized as the most well-regarded engineering school in the world (edging out MIT in a report they sponsored). Olin was cited for its "multidisciplinary student-centered education that extends across and beyond traditional engineering disciplines and is anchored in issues of ethics and social responsibility" (Graham, 2018).

Olin begins with hands-on challenges from Day One. Students engage in three dozen design-build projects culminating with a two-semester Senior Capstone in Engineering, where teams engage in impact projects with corporate partners, government research labs, nonprofits, and startups. If you visit at the end of a semester, you'll see students presenting a public product.

"No amount of emphasis on narrow specialized courses will produce the innovators we need," said Miller. What replaces narrow, specialized courses? Miller advocates for more global, complex, multidisciplinary challenges.

Education for the knowledge economy was about content transmission explained Miller—think instructor up front and students in rows and tests of knowledge. Education for the maker economy is about what you can do. Teachers are more guides on the side, and a lot of work is small-group maker

The Kern Entrepreneurial Engineering Network (KEEN) is a partnership of 47 leading universities with the shared mission "to graduate engineers with an entrepreneurial mindset" so they can go on to "create more personal, economic, and societal value through a lifetime of meaningful work" (Engineering Unleashed, n.d.b).

Unlike business schools, which often view entrepreneurship as a set of skills specific to starting a business, these engineering schools cultivate opportunity spotting and developing an impact-oriented mindset that could make a difference in a big company or social enterprise as well as a startup.

KEEN partners including Arizona State, Olin College, Colorado School of Mines (all features in this book) train young people to spot opportunities and use design skills for impact. They empower curiosity, help them make connections, and support design sprints where they can create value.

projects. Education for the emerging innovation economy is about what you can conceive. It's based on intrinsic motivation and design thinking and happens fluidly with peers and mentors (Miller, 2018).

Education for the innovation economy is not just about knowledge and skill, argues Miller; it's about mindset—collaborative, interdisciplinary, ethical, empathetic, entrepreneurial, and global. Developing these mindsets means an education that asks a new set of questions:

- Identity: who do you believe you are?

- Agency: what are you confident you can actually do?

- Purpose: how will your life make a positive difference?

Key to building these mindsets and being employable forever, as Miller suggests, is using design thinking to attack a series of increasingly complex problems. As evidenced at Design Tech High, embracing these new priorities requires new nimble structures with big blocks of time and collaboration across disciplines, new active learning roles for teachers and students, and new ways to report progress (for learners and institutions).

The KEEN network of engineering schools (featured above) focuses on entrepreneurial mindset—the ability to spot opportunity and deliver impact. They use design thinking (or computational thinking) as a created problem-solving approach. Both of these difference-making mindsets and skills require a well-developed sense of agency—the ability to manage attention, attitudes, actions, and the judgment to know what to learn and when to act.

Exercising Collaboration

Almost every significant contribution requires a team. That is increasingly true whether you're a doctor, entrepreneur, first responder, or educator. Every profession has moved beyond the individual craftsman to delivery in teams—and teams are often diverse in discipline, location, race, and levels of experience. Collaboration is the result of the intentional design of culture and structure; it's a set of agreements about tools and protocols; and it's the cultivation of individual mindsets and skill sets (Vander Ark & Liebtag, 2018).

The 200 schools in the New Tech Network share a commitment to team-taught–project-based learning in big blocks. These integrated blocks provide time to dive deep into complex topics and produce products valuable to the community. Students are assessed on collaboration and agency exhibited in each project. Most of the schools in the network are new or transformed district high schools that made a commitment to integrated project-based learning.

Marjory Stoneman Douglas Students Lead National Debate

Most students at Marjory Stoneman Douglas High School in Broward County, Florida, weren't planning on taking on the important issue of gun control, but they found a purpose and took control of the platform after a tragic school shooting in 2018. As evidenced by the incredible movement they started and led, they made a difference despite its origins in a terrible act of violence (Alter, 2018).

This experience was beyond traumatic for students and has led to many of them dedicating their lives since then to activism. Kai Koerber, who survived the events on February 14, started Societal Reform Corporation, a nonprofit dedicated to championing mental health, meditation, and mindfulness education. Koerber extends the opportunity for other young people to take action by starting their own societal reform clubs and spreading the word about how to make a difference. Students can get service learning hours for their contributions and commitments (Societal Reform Corporation, n.d.).

Design Thinking

Walking into Design Tech High on the Oracle Campus in Redwood City, California, many are immediately struck by how much the space and the activities *do not* look like school.

Right inside the front door is a huge shop called the Design Realization Garage (DRG) where Lead Science and Engineering Instructor Wayne Brock, a Purdue trained mechanical engineer, teaches a yearlong engineering course for juniors and seniors. About halfway through the course, students develop proposals for a final engineering project to demonstrate that they can add value for an external client group. "I include voice and choice in every assignment, moving from more constraints to less constraints," explained Brock (Getting Smart, 2020, January 2).

"We provide access to tools and materials, ranging from traditional woodworking to high-tech modern fabrication, such as three-dimensional printing and laser cutting. Students access the DRG through elective courses, design challenges, independent passion curiosity projects, and to make projects targeted at demonstrating competency in core courses," explained DRG

Director Galen McAndrew, the other half of the Design Tech maker team (Getting Smart, 2020, January 2).

McAndrew teaches prototyping to incoming freshmen. The semester-long course provides a survey of prototyping methods. One week you'll see students sketching ideas, the next week they'll be sewing, the following week, they'll be cutting and drilling wooden models—and learning to express their ideas in many ways.

The design thinking methodology used across the curriculum was inspired by the nearby Stanford d.school. It starts with empathy research to define a problem, then it shifts to idea creation, prototyping, and testing solutions. It is an iterative problem-solving approach particularly good for new and complex challenges.

Design thinking is as much a mindset as a methodology at Design Tech High. McAndrew explained that when writing an essay in English, students think deeply about the audience and iterate the message. With design thinking, says McAndrew, the school pushes students to think about problems and approaches that are constantly evolving, instead of the mindset that there's only one right answer.

The core values of trust, care, and creativity are evident in the culture, practices, schedules, and structures of Design Tech. It starts with a commitment to know each student personally, academically, culturally,

"51 It": Design Thinking at One Stone

Students at One Stone, a Boise high school and regional after school program, lead and tackle interesting problems. The work is rooted in design thinking, a human-centered creative problem-solving and innovation discovery process developed at Stanford University's d.school. At One Stone, they talk about "51ing it," which refers to the potential that it might take more than 50 iterations to get a solution right.

The 2019–2020 school year began with four-day Deep Dives, experiential learning opportunities that included solar energy, cybersecurity, mixing music, mindfulness, fly fishing, and filmmaking.

Coach Michael Reagan said most of the student-made films focused on topics students are passionate about. One involves a script that a student has been working on for years. Another deals with standing up to power dynamics, a third explores the challenges of aging. The goal is for students to go deep on something they are passionate about and to encourage them to think critically.

After Deep Dives came three weeklong immersions that allow more time out of the building. The weekly schedule also includes a 3-hour "Mission Block" for students to invest time on their own passion projects.

In the background of each experience are the 32 competencies that make up the school's Bold Learning Objectives: knowledge (how might we understand the world?), mindset (how might we practice with intention?), and creativity (how might we approach challenges?), and skills (how might we develop tools for life?). Artifacts from learning experiences are captured in a student-curated portfolio. Coach feedback is logged in a growth transcript that helps students describe their leadership and problem-solving capabilities.

Young people make up at least two-thirds of the nonprofit board—and they run very productive board meetings. The culture, as well as the structure, fosters students' voice and encourages difference making.

and cognitively and to use that knowledge to co-construct their learning experiences.

About 18 students meet with an advisor every day for 30 minutes. The research is clear said, Executive Director Ken Montgomery, the sustained mentorship of an advisory system is critical. On Thursdays, students create their own schedules with support from their advisors. The advisory system also supports the college awareness and application process.

Four times a year, Design Tech students take two intersession courses or do internships in areas they're passionate about. Some intersession courses are taught by Oracle employees and explore emerging technology.

Throughout their experience at Design Tech, students work on pressing problems and building transferable skills that will help them make a difference in the world, especially the senior engineering capstone focused on a proposal that students plan and create.

The leadership team at Design Tech High didn't start with classes and bell schedules; it started with a new mission: "We believe that the world can be a better place and that our students can be the ones to make it happen."

New Priorities Power Community Change

While young people live and work in a world full of novelty and complexity, most high schools value routine and compliance—small problems in repeated patterns with primary school behavior management systems. Developing leadership requires new priorities and new structures—introducing young people to successively larger challenges with more degrees of freedom. Like the gradual release that Wayne Brock described at Design Tech, it starts with skill building and adds voice and choice, and time and space to the challenges as student capabilities grow. Seniors at Design Tech are not only problem-solving, they are problem finding and then building solutions valuable to an external audience.

Real-World Learning Becomes New Priority in Kansas City

Over 100 high schools in 25 school districts in metropolitan Kansas City are embracing new priorities by putting real-world experiences at the center. Supported by the Kauffman Foundation, the Real-World Learning initiative is aimed at supporting and mobilizing community-connected learning. The goal is to add more powerful and relevant learning experiences and to help youth capture and communicate those experiences with credentials and assets recognized by higher education and employers. This has required leaders to shift their priorities.

The new opportunity is for every Kansas City student to graduate with market value assets including entrepreneurial experiences, client-connected projects, internships, college credit, and industry credentials. Across their experiences earning these assets, they will learn valuable skills that help them in life and work.

At Olathe West High, students in the Green Tech Academy built their own wind turbines, a farming robot, and an electric vehicle. Community-connected projects like these will be common across the metro area in the 2020–2021 school year.

There is no better way to develop agency and an entrepreneurial mindset than to engage in a series of extended community-connected challenges that result in valued public products.

For the last 20 years in America, standardized testing of grade level proficiency in reading and math has been the driving priority in education. Basic skills are obviously important, but the reductive mechanical view of school as test scores has damaged the profession of teaching and dehumanized the process of learning.

It's time for school communities to adopt new priorities relevant to the innovation economy, to help every learner develop the agency to lead and the curiosity and capability to take on high-impact problems. It's time to value the public products of difference making over test scores. It's time to help learners connect with a sense of purpose and build capabilities for difference making.

CHAPTER
FIVE

Purpose Powers Contribution

Having a sense of purpose is the long-term, number one motivator in life.

William Damon, Path to Purpose *(2010)*

To have purpose is to be engaged in something larger than the self, he said; it's often sparked by the observation that something's missing in the world that you might provide. It's also a mindset that many teenagers appear to lack, according to research Damon carried out at the Stanford Center on Adolescence: "About 20 percent of high school kids report being purposeful and dedicated to something besides themselves. The rest, or the majority [of high schoolers], are either adrift, frenetic with work but purposeless, or full of big dreams but lacking a deliberate plan."

Finding Purpose Through Farming

Leah Pinneman, former public school teacher now veteran and founding farmer of Soul Fire Farms in New York, decided over a decade ago that she needed to find her calling, a higher purpose. At age 16, she recalls an experience working at Boston's Food Project where she learned how to grow her own food. She spent time working in Ghana with farmers and community members. Pinneman decided she wanted to contribute to her people, current and of her ancestral past, and devote her life to "create spaces for people of color to heal and reconnect to the land" (Steinauer-Scudder, n.d.).

Her purpose became clear and from that a path to contributing in her community. Young professionals to soon-to-be retiring adults today are seeking this kind of purpose in their work. They don't look for jobs, they look for work that is meaningful—work that has purpose.

As Leah likely realized early on, your purpose—or what you are driven to do—might not immediately play to existing strengths and skills. Young people who identify their purpose might shy away from chasing their dreams or goals due to a fear that they aren't capable. We find in schools where learners are encouraged to pursue their purpose that they learn how to do the things they need, and willingly do, because they are incredibly motivated and connected to the outcome. Speaking in front of an audience might be the last thing a young person feels confident doing, but when the presentation of learning is tied to a cause the student cares about, they are more eager to take the risk and speak up.

The Baby Boomer generation created an extraction economy where wealth and possessions were the ultimate sign of success. Known as the "Me Generation," Boomers embraced individualism (Moody, n.d.). Tempered by the Great Recession, Millennials led the shift to a broader and more personal definition of success—a focus on personal fulfillment.

Purpose and personal fulfillment can lead to contribution. On the counter, contribution can lead to a sense of purpose. The combination, contribution with a sense of purpose, is life changing and world changing. This is the sweet spot, where passion and gifts meet a need or an opportunity (Robinson, 2014). "It is no accident that 'living purposely' is the sixth element of self-esteem" (hooks, 2001, p. 61).

In this chapter, we discuss

- The path to learners' finding their purpose as a priority in schools
- How school can be a place for students to find their calling through powerful projects and connected learning experiences

Contribution is for others. Purpose is personal. Young people can both pursue their own purpose and simultaneously find a way to contribute to the greater good. David Brooks calls it weaving, or "the spirit of caring you bring to each interaction with someone else. It's a willingness to be open and loving, whether you get anything in return" (Aspen Institute, n.d.). Three traits of a weaver:

> Contribution with a sense of purpose is life changing and world changing.

- A weaver views their community as home and tries to make it loving and welcoming

- A weaver treats neighbors as family regardless of outward differences

- A weaver finds meaning and joy in connection and caring for others

Purpose: Meaningful to Self, Consequential to the World

Project Wayfinder offers a yearlong high school curriculum focused solely on identifying purpose. It starts with getting curious about students' motivations. What do they care about? What excites them? What takes up most of their time and energy? What makes them mad? What problems do they want to solve?

The answer to these questions can provide clues to a sense of purpose. From there, it's up to educators to help connect the things students find purposeful to their educational experience and make explicit how succeeding in school can help students achieve the aspirations that matter most to them. This whole process starts by engaging authentically with students and asking meaningful questions.

Project Wayfinder is built around the idea, popularized by Stanford's William Damon, that purpose is something that is meaningful to self and consequential to the world. It presumes that purpose is dynamic and will evolve over time: "We encourage students to think of purpose as a non-linear and reflective process they can draw upon for guidance throughout their life" (Klein, 2019).

Project Wayfinder has been taught by over 1,000 teachers to more than 15,000 students at 200 schools worldwide.

"Imagine if schools adopted this strategy and gave students the resources and support to articulate their reasons for pursuing an education," said Director of Strategic Partnerships for Project Wayfinder Tim Klein. "We would see more engaged, resilient, and self-motivated students."

He added, "It's time to tap into the secret of peak performance and start asking them the most important question: Why?" (Klein, 2019)

On Calling

Sooner or later something seems to call us onto a particular path. You may remember this "something" as a signal moment in childhood when an urge out of nowhere, a fascination, a peculiar turn of events struck like an annunciation: This is what I must do, this is what I've got to have. This is who I am. (Hillman, 2017)

James Hillman, in his 2017 bestseller *The Soul's Code*, said, "Each person enters the world called." The idea may have originated with Plato and his Myth of Er, but there are plenty of stories from the Abrahamic tradition of responding to a call like Moses and the burning bush.

The idea of a unique calling is often tied to spiritual identity and, as a result, not prominent in psychological literature. But many educators felt the tug to teach early in life. Many doctors and nurses responded to the impulse to care and heal. Many pilots knew early that they needed to fly.

Musicians often find they can do no other than play music.

Joseph Campbell explained the response to your calling as following your bliss: "You put yourself on a kind of track, which has been there all the while, waiting for you, and the life that you ought to be living is the one you are living" (Joseph Campbell, 2019).

Authors Justine and Michael Toms (1999) suggest starting with pragmatic questions: Why am I here? What is the purpose of my life? Whom or what do I serve? How have I constructed my life to come to this place? What do I want to contribute to the world?

"If you don't have a clear answer to the question, never fear; it will emerge when the time is right and you are ready," they advise. They suggest that sometimes it will require experience, adventures, or challenges, to prepare us for the work we were meant to do.

A Systematic Approach to Calling

Learners in Cajon Valley Union School District experience 54 big integrated units of career education between kindergarten and eighth grade. Each unit includes projects connected to real-world problems. Students have the opportunity to explore, simulate, practice, and connect with industry experts.

After visiting a dam, middle school students conducted online research on dam construction, they built a three-dimensional model and created a video explanation. They conducted a video conference with engineers about water systems and wrote about the experience.

The district serves about 17,000 students in 10 elementary and middle schools northeast of San Diego. Nearly three-quarters of the students live in or near poverty and the region is home to many refugees.

With a mission of "happy kids, healthy relationships, in a path to gainful employment," the World of Work is the integrating framework for schools in Cajon. Periodically Cajon learners are prompted to ask, What are my strengths? What are my interests? What are my values? This enables them to check the fit with potential career pathways. The hard work of test-driving careers in elementary and middle school prepares Cajon learners to make informed choices in high school and beyond.

Passion as a Skill

The Toms explain that living into your call doesn't mean

> You should sit on the sidelines and wait for something to occur—quite the contrary. You're part of a creative process, and being able to follow your calling requires your active participation. Only then can you bring your gifts to the world.

At One Stone, they call passion a skill—something to be cultivated through the hard work of developing self-knowledge and immersing in the great issues of our time. It's the repeated effort of iterating issues and approaches to find the work that most speaks to you, which feels most valuable and fulfilling.

Finding this meaning and passion does not always happen in isolation. We seek connection and integrated experiences, yet school doesn't always provide these types of experiences for young people. Barumstier (1991) in *Meanings of Life*, shares: Although a life's meaning is quintessentially personal and individual, meaning itself is fundamentally social. Without culture—including language, value, and interpersonal relationships—life could not have much in the way of meaning (Baumeister, 1991, p. 6).

He reminds us that it is often finding a cause, a community, or a connection that is key to helping individuals identify their own purpose and way they want to make a difference. Of course, those who directly experience something—traumatic, life-changing (for better or worse), or profound, may take those events as foundational to why we want to make a difference.

Purpose comes with a connection and a deep-rooted understanding of why it matters to the young person. Education is to discover and develop capabilities for contribution and connect with purpose. Schools that educate for purpose find learning and student work focused on difference making inevitable.

Communities of Contribution

There is no power for change greater than a community discovering what it cares about.

—*Margaret J. Wheatley (2010)*

Entire communities need to rally behind change in our schools and empowering young people to help be a part of building a better future. What if we asked children about their dream machine—and then helped them build it? A Belgian boy named Oskar wanted a machine to dig for Roman treasure. He made a drawing and wrote a user manual. His father wasn't very handy but didn't dismiss his request. They went to a technical school and talked to engineers. And soon, MyMachine was born.

MyMachine Global, a community-based program, invites elementary students to describe their dream machine. College design students and high school prototypers help bring to life the dreams of elementary students. MyMachine has spread across Belgium and now supports programs in eight countries (T. Vander Ark, 2018, July 17).

"MyMachine combines different aspects of entrepreneurship like creativity, motivation and taking initiative," said Bernard De Potter, administrator of the Flemish Agency of Innovation and Entrepreneurship which sponsored MyMachine across Belgium. "But the most valuable aspect is that children and students learn through experience and concrete activity: from the idea of a dream machine of children in primary schools, over the concept of students in higher education towards the real machine built by students in secondary education" (2018, July 17).

Young people spend a great deal of time in school, but we often neglect the other important parts of their community experiences and upbringing and that are formative learning. Faith congregations, Boys and Girls Club, after-school programs, and organizations such as MyMachine all have influence on the students they serve.

There are countless examples of community-based organizations and efforts aimed at developing youth and empowering difference making. This chapter reviews examples in leadership and service; technology and design; health, food, and nature; entrepreneurship; and the arts.

In this chapter, we discuss

- Programs and community organizations that help youth learn to make a difference in their own lives or the lives of others.
- Categories of difference making include leadership and service; technology and design; health, food, and nature; entrepreneurship; and the arts.

Leadership and Service

Senior capstone projects, common in high schools, engage about-to-be-graduates in taking on a community challenge. They often include service to the community and leadership development for the student. Programs that extend access to community-connected learning opportunities like these in and out of school are becoming more popular. Outside organizations can be key partners for schools in creating these types of experiences and offering them more frequently and for a prolonged period of time.

Organizations can be the backbone of support for many students and understand their needs just as much as a school can. Strong partnerships with schools can lead to more students getting what they need and finding avenues where they want to engage in community service and develop leadership skills.

The Service Learning Project, one such example, creates opportunities for Brooklyn youth to become active citizens in their schools and communities. Through school day and after-school programs, young people become agents of change in the community (Pitofsky, 2019).

YouthBuild focuses on leadership development for unemployed, out-of-school youth to help build opportunities for them to gain skills they need for employment and become leaders in their communities. The hope is that youth become impact-driven leaders and gain meaningful work and employment, which is better to the world. Germain Castellanos, YouthBuild graduate, shared, "Giving back to the community helped me become a different person, it transformed my life completely—through YouthBuild" ("YouthBuild Stories," n.d.).

The Future Is Mine provides career expiration opportunities for 700 students annually from 26 western Pennsylvania high schools. The program from the Consortium for Public Education allows students to work on team projects that connect them with employers in the community while developing skills they'll need to be successful in the workplace—from organization and planning to communications and collaboration.

The KidsRights Changemaker Program also provides leadership opportunities for youth to develop a project, start fundraising, and share their dreams (KidsRights Changemakers, n.d.). Students can start their own project ideas or support the development of another existing project. Over 147 projects from around the world are available to engage in on the site. Honored in 2019 with the International Children's Peace Prize, Divina Maloum developed Children for Peace (C4P) to help warn and educate children in Cameroon about enrollment in armed groups. She has organized peace clubs and camps to counter violent extremism and recruitment of children by related groups (KidsRights Changemakers, 2019).

Promoting Dignity for All

Global Dignity is an organization dedicated to teaching children worldwide how to "tap into values of kindness, understanding, tolerance, and compassion." The organization is dedicated to building a broader, participatory, ground-up movement for justice, equality, and peace. Global Dignity Day, an annual event focused on dignity, has generated countless projects and movements around the world dedicated to bringing more dignity to their communities (Walton, 2018, February, 27).

Learner experiences provided on the site encourage young people to take action and choose a project they want to work on that has local or global impact (Walton, 2018, October 15). Over 860,000 recorded young people from more than 70 countries participated in Global Dignity Day in 2018.

Honorary Global Dignity Board Member Archbishop Desmond Tutu spoke on Dignity Day in 2011 of the importance of committing to making a difference to benefit others. He said, " . . . in our part of the world we speak of something called Ubuntu. The essence of being human. We say a person is a person through other persons. I need you to be all you can be, so that I can be I can be. You, you, you . . . all of you my children are members of one family" (Global Dignity, 2017).

One of the core principles relates directly to difference making in communities and to Tutu's point: "Has the responsibility to create the conditions for others to fulfill their potential, acting to strengthen the dignity of others, building a foundation of freedom, justice and peace for this, and future generations."

Other community initiatives put student passions and purpose front and center, whether partnered with a school on community service or not. The Purpose Project, incubated by IDEO, is a curriculum and digital platform that helps young people use design thinking to develop their purpose through impact projects.

Global Citizen Year places high school graduates in nine-month service projects around the world to support difference making. Abby Falik ("Podcast: Abby Falik on the Benefits of Global Service," 2019) created the gap year program to give young people an immersive cultural experience and success in serving a community. Alumni are curious, courageous, more willing to do the hard things that matter.

Outside of community service and leadership, another common focus of community-based organizations is on technology and design for good.

Technology and Design

Technological advancements including smart tools and billions of sensors have increased our ability to see where change is needed. Technologies we take for granted today, such as geographic information systems and global positioning systems, have dramatically increased our ability to spot a problem and quickly collect data to start addressing what to do about it.

There is a big data set behind every problem. It's becoming easier to collect and analyze data to streamline worldwide shipping logistics, or estimate how much plastic is dumped into the ocean each day, or review a billion images in search of cancer cells, or translate documents from one orphaned language to another.

Similarly, design has emerged as a skill not just for graphic artists and engineers but as a tool for addressing new and complex problems and delivering value. Community organizations are realizing the potential of both technology and design to equip young people to be world shapers. The ability to design and data strategies to address problems are durable and transferable skills in the innovation economy.

Launched by the faculty and staff of Stanford, AI4ALL is a summer program for high school students who self-identify as part of an underrepresented group. By connecting them to computer scientists from 16 leading universities, youth learn to use Artificial Intelligence (AI) to solve problems they care about. In 2019, they launched open tools for difference making. The free 30-hour curriculum can be incorporated into a class, a club, or a workshop.

AI Solutions Driven by Community and Family Designs

Tara C. Chklovski grew up in a small town outside Delhi. Inspired by a tinkering father, Tara wanted to be an aerospace engineer. After earning a master's degree at Boston University, Tara launched into a Ph.D. at USC. But the pull to help more girls experience powerful science, engineering, and technology education drew her away. In 2006, she formed nonprofit Technovation and launched the Artificial Intelligence (AI) Family Challenge. Families learn about AI and use it to solve a problem in their community.

Five design challenges introduce families to AI concepts. Three more design challenges explore robotics. Ten more lessons prepare families to solve a problem in their communities and submit to the AI World Championship. The AI Family Challenge works on a platform using Machine Learning for Kids, which builds on IBM Watson and contributes to Scratch, a widely used educational coding platform.

Technovation Girls has chapters around the world and sponsors an annual technology challenge that thousands of girls participate in (Getting Smart, 2019).

On an even bigger scale, Design for Change cultivates a mindset of "I can" make a difference in every student and creates impact champions around the world.

On a global scale, Design for Change cultivates an "I can" mindset and equips children "to be aware of the world around them enabled with the skills to take action and empowered to design a more desirable and sustainable future." Fueled by an online database of projects for students to participate in, Design for Change empowers schools and communities to use the Sustainable Development Goals as an opportunity for students to engage in generating solutions (Design for Change, n.d.). Over 30,000 solutions have been submitted to Design for Change and added to their "i CAN" marketplace ("Design for Change i CAN marketplace," n.d.). Solutions submitted from schools around the world range from ways to feed the hungry to cleaner water technologies. Howard Gardner and his team at Harvard Project Zero researched the impact and found "clear improvements in student empathy as well as challenges in enhancing problem-solving abilities" ("Design for Change Research," n.d.).

DoSomething is another initiative that has big ambitions for how technology can power difference making. Their goal is to mobilize young people in every American area code and in 131 countries. Young people can sign up to volunteer, help create social change, or initiate civic action campaigns to make a real-world impact on causes that the young person cares about. Similarly, the Better Their World Student Project Database is a free curated list of completed real-world projects with measurable impact on the world (The Better Their World Student Project Database, n.d.).

Health, Food, and Nature

There is some evidence that the health and well-being of young people in the United States and other developed nations has declined over the last two decades. New pressures and less predictable pathways contribute more uncertainty. Depression has become increasingly common among American youth—especially teen girls (Geiger & Davis, 2019). Teen suicides increased 56% from 2007 to 2017 (Curtin & Heron, 2019). Young people who have experienced adverse family circumstances such as trauma, abuse, and neglect have poorer health outcomes. A variety of community organizations are engaging young people to improve health and wellness.

Big Green is building a national school food culture that promotes youth wellness. Through food literacy programs and a network of Learning Gardens, students, parents, and teachers are connected through robust food culture. They are focused on underserved schools in seven cities. Their high school programs help students launch food-based businesses using produce from their gardens (C. Vander Ark, 2019).

Green Bronx Machine is focused on growing healthier communities, particularly those in the New York City area. The idea is that to grow healthier students and communities, you have to start by having them develop solutions that directly benefit them and 100% of society. Green Bronx teaches students to grow healthy foods in their own neighborhoods and envision "a world where people do not have to leave their community to live, learn and earn in a better one" (Green Bronx Machine, n.d.).

Document Your Place on the Planet, an effort from the Global Oneness Project, provides learners the opportunity to contribute a photograph or some form of media highlighting their place and perspective about climate breakdown and role on this earth. While students may or may not already be engaged directly in a project to provide a solution or contribute to a community, the project asks: How might schools serve students by highlighting their perspectives and actions? The hope is that schools, educators, and students will embrace this challenge and document how they see the world, both its beauty and its destruction with climate breakdown (Global Oneness Project, n.d.).

In 2008, college student Seth Maxwell and six friends in Southern California learned that more than a billion people didn't have access to safe, clean drinking water. They raised money and funded a well for an African community. When they realized that no one was activating youth around the water issue, they created ThirstProject. Ten years later, they have equipped thousands of students in hundreds of schools and colleges to join the fight. They have raised over $10 million for more than 3,000 clean water projects.

Take Action Global (TAG) works with schools to take action on social good causes including the United Nations Sustainable Development Goals. TAG helps schools develop Innovation Labs and Clubs to promote difference making. TAG organizes an annual Climate Action project to promote issues exploration and solution development.

CISCO is recognizing young people who are leading in ways that promote the global goals. Partnered with Global Citizen, an organization and growing movement aimed at eradicating poverty by 2039, together they launched the Global Citizen Prize: Cisco Youth Leadership Award. The award honors "someone who can demonstrate the achievement of measurable impact at scale over the last three to five years and who has advanced one or more of the Global Goals, while inspiring other young people to do the same" (Global Citizen, n.d.).

Entrepreneurship

More than three quarters of a million businesses were launched in the United States in 2019, up nearly 40% since the Great Recession (Statista, 2019). Whether starting a business, exploring gig and freelance opportunities, or looking for ways to add value from inside a larger organization, we're all entrepreneurs in the innovation economy. Unfortunately, entrepreneurship hasn't made its way into high school graduation requirements just yet. Fortunately, though, a growing number of community organizations have put making a difference at the heart of how students can use entrepreneurship skills.

Dual School supplements a high school curriculum by creating a safe place for Delaware students to work on social impact projects they care about. After the kickoff weekend, Dual School students meet weekly for three hours for 10 weeks. Founder Zachary Jones is the author of *The World Changer's Handbook: A Young Person's Guide to Creating an Impactful Life*.

Founded by Indiana teacher Don Wettrick, The STARTedUP Foundation empowers student entrepreneurs and innovators with collaborative, immersive experiences, accelerator programs, and the first seed fund for students under 20 ("Don Wettrick on Teaching Entrepreneurship," 2019).

Based in San Diego with locations in St. Louis, Austin, and New York City, Whatever it Takes (WIT) is a six-unit college credit social entrepreneur and leadership program in the country. Also headquartered in San Diego, Real World Scholars EdCorps Program operates an e-commerce platform that allows students to develop and operate businesses under their nonprofit umbrella.

Startable Pittsburgh is a free program that teaches high school students entrepreneurial and maker skills. Students work in teams to design, prototype, build, brand, and market products of their own creation. Participants earn a stipend, keep all profits from their products, and pitch for more funding at our final event.

The Possible Project provides young people in Boston and Cambridge entrepreneurship experiences and the support and structures to start their own businesses or help grow an existing one (Possible Project, n.d.). The student-run businesses tie to student interests or a need in the community. Students who complete the program are eligible for college credit.

The Arts

Public expression and displays of art often represent or bring to light a cause or person who has made a difference in a community. Young people in schools all over the world are creating compassionate works of art that connect their love for music, murals, or other media to difference making. Whether they are telling the story of a powerful changemaker and it ignites their own desire to contribute in some way or they are creating a representation of an initiative they were a part of, art is an incredibly powerful vehicle for doing good.

Producing Films Focused on Making a Difference

Youth Cinema Project, an initiative of the Latino Film Institute, is flourishing in Santa Ana Unified School District (SAUSD). Students create, write, direct, and produce films, which are often about their community or a local challenge their community is facing. They contribute films that highlight their stories, their families, and their voices and work with leading filmmakers (a group of intentionally culturally diverse filmmakers) to receive guidance and support.

Students as early as third and fourth grades create and produce high-quality films. Genevieve Lunt, one of the first teachers to help pilot this program at Heninger Elementary School, worked with former SAUSD leader David Haglund to implement the work. In particular, Genevieve and Haglund knew this would be an incredible opportunity for the SAUSD population, who are predominantly Latino and English Language Learners. The film project allows students to choose what they want to write about and how they want to share their stories and, by nature of producing a film, encourages language development.

The film concept was developed by Edward James Olmos and the Latino Film Institute. The culminating or capstone courses at the high school level in SAUSD are offered in conjunction with the Dodge Film School at Chapman University. SAUSD film students have access to several full tuition scholarships at Chapman, which are accessible to those who complete the film pathway. After producing a film, students often continue to work on the cause and make a difference (Liebtag, 2017, April 24).

Youth Express is an Internet radio service featuring original writing, journalism, and reflections from Pittsburgh youth. Featured content includes student talk shows, poetry slams, and writing done for class assignments, school newspapers, or personal interest.

Throughout the city of Durham, North Carolina, 14 murals of Pauli Murray cover walls and buildings downtown. As a poet, attorney, activist, and Episcopal priest, Murray worked to address injustice, to give voice, to educate, and to promote reconciliation. Students from local elementary schools worked alongside over 1,500 community members to complete the murals and learn about Murray's impact on the world ("Pauli Murray Project," n.d.; BullCity Schools, 2019).

Thinking Big in Dallas

Big Thought is a 30-year-old Dallas nonprofit attacking the opportunity gap by bringing creative opportunities to youth that need them most.

Thriving Minds is an after-school program where teaching artists guide young people in creative experiences.

Through after-school clubs and curriculum, DaVerse helps middle and high school students find their voice. Several times each year, students from around the region present live music, art, and spoken word productions at a local venue.

Creative Solutions is an arts-as-workforce intervention program for adjudicated youth. An opportunity advisor engages youth in the arts, helps channel resiliency, explores possible futures, and connects youth to resources. The trauma-informed program culminates in a big musical production or gallery display. Sponsoring municipalities save money because the program reduces recidivism.

With a focus on creativity and an array of art rich programs, "We're confronting radical differences in opportunity," said Executive Director Byron Sanders.

"It's time to stop asking kids what they want to be in the future; why do they have to wait? They have the agency and power to make a difference right now."

These organizations and initiatives all are engaging youth in making a mark on their community through art. All of these programs build creativity and agency. Some connect with meaningful career pathways. The coming social economy may help unlock new ways to get paid for contributing to the common good.

The Emerging Social Economy

The programs highlighted above do an admirable job of engaging youth in volunteer service activities. Some of the college programs highlighted in Chapter 9 prepare youth for what have been considered service professions. For hundreds of years we have thought about contribution as service employment or volunteer activities. The coming social economy will better recognize, value, and reward contributions to the common good.

The shifting nature of employment sets the stage for the social economy. A growing proportion of workers are engaged in short-term employment, often called gig work. This includes independent contractors, online platform workers, contract firm workers, on-call workers, and temporary workers. In 2020, more than four in ten American workers did full- or part-time gig work (International Labour Organization, n.d.). Ridesharing apps Uber and Lyft may be the most visible gig work platforms, but a large number of workers find short gigs on Craigslist, Thumbtack, TaskRabbit, and Upwork. For skilled professionals, sometimes referred to as freelancers, digital staffing platforms can be a flexible and lucrative way to provide short-term services. For some, gig work offers valuable supplementary income earned on a flexible schedule. For most, gig work is relatively unstable low wage employment without health or retirement benefits.

The digital platforms that spurred the growth of gig work created new business models, new trust agreements (e.g., getting into a stranger's car), and new payment mechanisms. This infrastructure, with two developments, is the foundation for the emerging social economy of people helping people.

The first important development is better measurement of contribution—not just time but value created. The 40,000 Airbnb experiences illustrate this shift from time to value. The experiences include cooking classes, animal encounters, live music, tours, and adventures. With ratings and differential pricing, they encourage social entrepreneurs to deliver quality creative and learning experiences.

The second development will be broader reimbursement for services and payments that reflect contribution. There appears to be a rising sense of mutuality brought about by the rolling shocks of pandemics, natural disasters, and economic dislocations. This new mutuality is reinforced by a broadening consensus that widening income inequality is unsustainable and that new sharing mechanisms for the extraordinary benefits of the innovation economy are required. As a result of these sudden shocks and the slow build of a new consensus, regional and national governments will expand support for youth and family services and paid service opportunities, which would dampen the impacts of dislocation but expand opportunities for contribution. Expanded access to well-paying service opportunities in areas such as public art and elder care is also an alternative to or supplement for a universal basic income, which many argue will be required to cope with innovation economy dislocation.

The social economy will be a source of creative employment as well as contribution. Workforce development boards and social service agencies could work together to identify service opportunities. A public incubator could help social entrepreneurs assemble and test contribution experiences. Lifelong service opportunities will also require access to lifelong learning and guidance services—which themselves will grow as service opportunities.

Engaging middle and high school students in the service economy builds their social network. In her 2018 book, *Who You Know*, Julia Freeland Fisher argues that helping youth build social capital is critical to expanding equitable opportunity (Getting Smart, 2018, September 13). Fisher advocates for extended and outside of school learning opportunities, including those where students are making a difference in their communities. It is often these connections and contributions that differentiate them from another young person trying to get a job or a degree.

For some, building social capital and creating a culture and curriculum of contribution may cut against the grain of the American tradition of personal identity and autonomy. It's less familiar than the pursuit of individual gain. But ironically, it's clear that contribution is the superpower of the innovation economy. It is learning how to make a difference that builds value for individuals and communities.

Schools around the world are realizing the potential of focusing on difference making. Some build it into their mission. Some create partnerships with organizations discussed in this chapter. They become schools alive with possibility.

PART THREE

Difference Making

Schools Alive With Possibility

We can change the world and make it a better place. It is in our hands to make a difference.

—*Nelson Mandela*

Most schools have focused on compliance more than contribution. However, many educators are working hard to rewrite and redefine what school is and what learning looks like. Our new history is one of promise and possibility.

In Part III, we outline a brief history of schooling in the United States and begin to describe the new narrative that is forming. We then share examples of schools around the world paving the way and developing solution-minded students. Every student, no matter where they go to school, deserves these types of opportunities and experiences.

There is no lack of possibility, just a lack of enough progress for all. We highlight K–12 schools that are alive with possibility and difference makers. We provide examples of how their leadership priorities embrace making a difference and demonstrate the outcomes they have seen as a result of these shifts.

Colleges are beginning to embrace the idea of difference making as well. We provide examples of postsecondary programs and institutions working toward new aims and contribution.

We close Part III and the book by encouraging anyone working with youth to focus on the ideas we presented in the book and to do it with a sense of urgency.

A New History

We sort them by age, not aptitude; govern learning by bells, not mastery;
teach to the test, not to their interests.

—*Joseph South, ISTE (2018)*

Isabella took English, Biology, and Algebra 1, as a high school freshman. She used a flashcard app to memorize body parts for the physiology test. She memorized procedures so that she could factor polynomials on a math quiz. As a sophomore in Austin, Isabella memorized the symbols for the elements on the periodic table in Chemistry. In World History, she memorized dates of important events to ace the final. She took Physics as a junior (because 10 academics in 1892 decided it should come last even though parts of it are fundamental to Biology and Chemistry) along with Algebra 2 because that's what comes after Geometry (another American anachronism) and U.S. History. Isabella got good grades in school because her mom and dad told her that was important for getting into a good college—and that proved to be the case. As a senior, she was accepted to a number of selective universities. She mastered the game of school and it paid off.

Kylin, on the other hand, was an off-track teen in Columbus. He had no reason to go to school, including a long list of suspensions and teachers who didn't know what to do with him. It wasn't until his last chance, a program called Options for Success, that Kylin connected with learning. Rather than teaching math and marketing as a lecture style class, the teachers at Options for Success, brought Kylin and several teammates to a local restaurant where they worked with the owner to plan a second location. Through this project and others, Kylin learned the essentials of marketing, accounting, and investing. He discovered his strengths, developed his leadership skills, and learned that he could make a difference in his community. The experience motivated Kylin to continue on and earn an industry recognized credential (Korda, 2019). The difference between the experiences these two students had is dramatic.

About 15 million young people attend high school in the United States and, such as Isabella, nearly all of them take a series of required classes organized by disciplines. They learn stuff to pass a test, get a grade, and earn a diploma. They hope that diploma gets them to a university that four years later might have enough relevance to earn them a job.

In this chapter, we discuss

- A brief history of schooling in the United States and current paradigms
- Emerging alternatives in goals and structures for learning

Mass access to a high school education was the escalator to the American Dream. The escalator doesn't work very well anymore. It has never worked very well for young people from low-income households. And now it is clear the escalator falls short of giving young people a good start.

Organizing secondary schools around discipline-based courses facilitates staffing with a modicum of expertise, but it prevents young people from working on big, interesting problems like the restaurant expansion project that renewed Kylin's interest in school. These can be the most valuable experiences young people have.

Most high school assignments are discrete tasks with right answers—something that almost never happens in real life. And, for the last 20 years, most high schools have focused exclusively on preparing for college—an extension of the isolated discipline-based abstracted world.

Courses have been the organizing framework of secondary and postsecondary education for hundreds of years. The Committee of Ten in 1892 set standards for courses. With a strong equity impulse, the committee recommended that "every subject which is taught at all in a secondary school should be taught in the same way and to the same extent to every pupil so long as he pursues it, no matter what the probable destination of the pupil may be, or at what point his education is to cease" (T. Vander Ark, 2019, March 15). That list of required courses has driven the master schedule of almost every high school in the world ever since. And, as a result, students have been shuffling from one unrelated course to another every hour for more than a century.

As the organizing premise for high school and college, courses have several shortcomings. They value seat time rather than more accurate measures of human capability. They inhibit authentic, community-connected, and integrated approaches to addressing real problems. They limit divergence in modality or path and are often idiosyncratic in content and grading.

Some districts and networks have imposed a common curriculum—often complete with lesson plans, instructional materials, and pacing guides—to gain consistency within the course structure and to attempt to monitor for quality. This deals with only one of the problems with courses and may decrease the attractiveness of teaching. The other way to force course consistency is common end-of-course assessments. The problem with this approach is that you get what you test.

Discipline-based courses are a relic of education as knowledge transmission. Today, knowledge is freely available and what's important is how you combine it with skills to deliver value. A list of courses will not help young people in high school or college find and begin to make their unique contributions. The implicit goals of high school may have been beneficial for the industrial age—attending required classes, being quiet, passing standardized tests—but they promote compliance rather than leadership and innovation.

Education as knowledge transmission may go back to Plato. "At the core," argues Arizona State Professor Sasha Barab, "is an educational system heavily influenced by dualist assumptions inherent in the works of Plato, making it seem reasonable if not expeditious to build lessons focused on transmitting abstracted universals into a learner's disembodied mind."

Boredom may be the biggest challenge we face in modern high schools. Nearly half of middle and high students in a Gallup poll reported being either not engaged or actively disengaged in school (2016 Gallup Student Poll, 2017). A Yale study (2020) reported that high school students have negative feelings most of the time. In open-ended responses, about 80 percent reported feeling stressed and almost 70 percent said they were bored.

The combination of stress and boredom may be a result of trying to push content they don't care about into their brains. In a world where consent matters, pushing content into another brain seems like the wrong metaphor. "Maybe we should focus on learning as a process of invitation, not intervention," said Barab.

Organizing School Around Skill Sprints, Dialogs, and Projects

"We believe each person who enters Acton Academy will find a calling that changes the world."

The small K–12 Austin school offers a big promise that through Socratic dialogs and experiential learning each member of the Acton community will begin a Hero's Journey; discover precious gifts and a commitment to mastery; become a curious, independent, lifelong learner; embrace the forging of a strong character; cherish the arts, the physical world, and the mysteries of life; and treasure economic, political, and religious freedom.

The robust promise has activated the Austin microschool for a decade, Acton Academy is now the flagship of a global school network with more than 185 partners in 30 states and 20 countries.

Younger students have big morning blocks for individual work on core skills—reading, writing, and math. Goal setting, points, and badges motivate progress. A suite of adaptive tools support individual progress on skill development.

Acton learners practice critical thinking and powerful writing and speaking through deep Socratic discussions about heroes, history, and self-governance. They are asked to make and defend difficult real-world decisions building habits and mindsets that forge character.

A big afternoon block gives learners a chance to take on quests—challenging hands-on projects that give Acton learners the opportunity to apply skills. The four- to six-week projects are bounded by a compelling narrative and designed to deliver 21st-century skills.

Acton is a leading example of purposeful education that is both student-centered and character-based and one organized around skill sprints, projects, and dialogs rather than discipline-based courses (T. Vander Ark, 2019, August 26).

He argues that the core value exchange—learn this stuff and I'll give you a grade—is just a bad bargain. Barab suggests a thought experiment, what if we started with the learner and what they care about?

Fortunately, there are a growing number of alternatives that do. "As I travel the country, I encounter examples of schools where nearly every student is fully engaged and excited to be there," said Joseph South, ISTE. "Where student and teacher agency is respected, supported, and rewarded, engagement skyrockets" (South, 2018).

A Return to Place and Purpose

For many, the history of schooling in the United States is a lesson in what *not* to do. South is amongst a growing number of educators who realize the promise and possibility of new alternatives. There are signs and significant evidence that things have been changing and a revolution is stirring. In 2019 alone, hundreds of thousands of teachers went on strike to advocate for better pay but also for the right to shift to new priorities and crawl out of the testing era. They went on strike for better quality instruction and 21st-century environments, taking a stand that old priorities are now obsolete and not serving students well (Wong, 2019).

Change has been happening outside of school buildings and in community-based organizations, churches, and businesses—pushing the education system to give and shift. Towns and cities are feeling the economic shifts and impact from shortcomings of our past and advocating for better for our young people.

Grace Lee Boggs, educator and activist, empowered change in Detroit communities after experiencing decades of turmoil in her city, an era of testing and closing schools. "In order to transform our children . . . into positive change agents, our schools need to give them a sense of the unique capacity of human beings to shape and create reality in accordance with conscious purposes and plans" (Boggs, 2012, p. 137).

Boggs, amongst many others, realized the potential of schooling that transforms and creates agents of change rather than vessels for consumption. Detroit is a perfect example of a city that needs a generation of young people who care about making a difference.

The Boggs School was formed to honor her work and continues to engage elementary-aged students in activities to fulfill their mission, focused on difference making: "The mission of the Boggs School is to nurture creative, critical thinkers who contribute to the well-being of their communities" ("Boggs Center," n.d.).

Organizations and efforts like the Southeast Michigan Stewardship Coalition (SEMIS), inspired by Boggs's work, are working in tandem with school communities to advance this agenda. Their mission is ". . . empowering youth to become 'solutionaries' capable of improving the health of human and natural environments" ("Southeast Michigan Stewardship Coalition," n.d.).

A growing number of schools around the world are embracing these kinds of ideas and returning to communities to do deep work focused on making a difference locally. Schools are engaging young people in solution-building and finding their purpose.

Can Schools Help Create a Post-Capitalist World?

Gregory Smith of Antioch College writes in his article "Can Schools Help Create a Post-Capitalist World?":

> An education aimed at preparing people to take orders from others, complete often meaningless tasks, and consume is not likely to cultivate the forms of intelligence, responsibility, and activism demanded by the future. However, in a small but growing number of schools in North America, Europe, Australia, New Zealand, and Japan, educators are experimenting with approaches to teaching and learning that are preparing the young for a different kind of interaction with their society, an interaction premised on thoughtful problem-solving and participation.

> Grounding learning in knowledge and issues central to the health of the human and natural communities surrounding the school, these educators are finding ways to induct their students into an understanding of the interconnections that link different disciplines and phenomena, and the role citizens can play in preserving, maintaining, and restoring the integrity and stability of these communities. In doing so, they are contributing to the sustainability, resilience, and self-renewal of the social and ecological systems that undergird human welfare and security. (Smith, 2012, p. 4)

Throughout the 30-year standards-based reform movement and preoccupation with standardized testing, hundreds of schools, many working in networks, focused on deeper learning flourished. With roots in Ted Sizer's Coalition of Essential Schools (formed in 1984), they use project-based learning to engage young people in authentic work that matters to them and their communities. Convened by the Hewlett Foundation in 2010, Deeper Learning networks (featured in this book) include Big Picture Learning, EL Education, High Tech High, and New Tech Network.

These Deeper Learning networks maintained the century-old active hands-on learning tradition espoused by John Dewey and added design thinking, internships, and leadership opportunities. They laid the groundwork for next-generation school design initiatives, such as XQ Superschool (six XQ schools are featured in this book), which focus on difference making.

From compliance, control, and testing, new priorities such as agency, design thinking, and entrepreneurship are surfacing in school systems across the country. Our communities, educators, and places of work are demanding a better learning experience for young people.

Our history of schooling precedes us, but it does not have to define our future. The next chapter features 17 high schools where young people are helping to create the future and creating new approaches to teaching and learning.

CHAPTER
EIGHT

Contribution at the Core

You cannot get through a single day without having an impact on the world around you. What you do makes a difference, and you have to decide what kind of difference you want to make.

—*Jane Goodall*

Kate Reed hated her traditional high school. She lasted about two weeks. When she found NuVu Studio, she knew it was a fit. At her new school, Reed and two colleagues designed a hand drive that could snap onto the free wheel of a chair. After some tinkering, they determined they could make it work on both sides of the chair and backwards as well as forwards. They developed an inexpensive 3D printable version. The team was invited to show its invention to the White House Science Fair. President Obama tested the device and was impressed by the concept.

NuVu Studio is a micro school, which is a school with fewer students and can sometimes be located within another larger school, for example, on Cambridge Avenue halfway between Harvard and MIT with several other campuses around the world. The small secondary school uses the city as the classroom and encourages students to use a design process to solve complex challenges using creativity, critical thinking, and collaboration—producing real impact for real audiences.

As the first NuVu graduate in 2017, Reed is continuing her design studies as an awarded scholar at the Rhode Island School of Design. About her projects at NuVu, Reed said, "I can code, I can create things, I can do art, I can do technology. There is nothing stopping me here. I always realized I had the spark and that excitement to learn but before I wasn't given the chance to grow, but project after project I see myself through a different lens and see the impact I can make" (NuVu Studio, 2016).

"We want students to have experiences as they create these projects that are unlike anything they have ever experienced before. Their learning should feel original and challenge them to think of new ideas," shared founder Saeed Arida (Liebtag, 2019, April 8).

The studio model that NuVu offers provides students with the opportunity to problem-solve through creating and building. The curriculum at NuVu is based on the architectural studio model. Students are presented with an open-ended topic and, within a two-week studio framework, they work collaboratively among themselves to create both a problem and a solution.

Studios are multidisciplinary and may require data analytics, robotics, coding, communication, fabrication, electronic, and other maker skills. Through these applied and integrated learning experiences, students have the opportunity to create, make, and build. At Nuvu, the product is important, but it's more about how you attack complex problems, incorporate feedback, and persevere to find solutions.

Like NuVu, schools alive with possibility make contribution the priority with big blocks of time and support for work that is connected to the community.

In this chapter, we discuss

- How equity and difference making can be at the heart of a school mission
- Eight case studies of schools that feature extended challenges and use design thinking to address real-world problems
- How educators can begin to shift their practice and access difference-making opportunities for themselves

Difference Making as the Priority

This book proposes a new equity bargain, one where all young people are valued for their gifts and interests and their unique opportunity to contribute to their community. The purpose of education in the innovation economy is to equip and initiate contribution.

Nuvu is one of the growing number of schools prioritizing difference making. Another purpose-built school opened in the last decade is NOLA Micro Schools, an Acton Academy affiliate in New Orleans. Founder Kim Gibson said, "Every one of our students will find a calling, something they love and are good at."

A typical day at NOLA Micro begins and ends with a Socratic discussion where a teacher serves as a guide, setting up scenarios, and asking questions to stimulate critical thinking and independent learning. After independent skill building, students engage in real-world group projects. That might include starting a business, publishing a book, or building a wind turbine. The purpose of the school is to help every student find a calling and change the world. The school is small but the goal is audacious.

Liger Leadership Academy of Cambodia is another purpose-built school developed in the last 10 years. The small secondary school is "committed to nurturing highly-skilled entrepreneurial thinkers who are globally-minded, determined, ethical, passionate, and effective." Liger is based on the premise that one student can make a big difference in the world.

"Liger students aren't waiting for tomorrow; they are changing their country now," said founders Trevor and Agnieszka Gile. The key shift in mindset is from education as preparation—as a prophylactic for some future inevitability—to education as contribution. All of the Liger students are involved in projects improving Cambodia. Three quarters of students are published authors.

> I made a documentary about my classmates expressing their feelings toward the Cambodian Genocide Museum and the Khmer Rouge regime. It makes me happy that the documentary impacts audiences when it is shown in different places. I really want to become a filmmaker and impact people's perspectives, said Liger senior Samaday. ("Liger Leadership Academy," n.d.)

At High Tech High, a K–12 school network in San Diego, projects integrate hands and minds across multiple disciplines and culminate in the creation of meaningful and beautiful work. Students engage in work that matters to them, their peers, and the community. The tradition of outstanding student publications starts in elementary school, with examples like a field guide to San Diego County birds and native plants written by third graders.

Amazing student artwork from integrated projects is displayed in each of the High Tech High campuses reinforcing a culture of quality work for public audiences.

Time and Support for Difference Making

Good schools have intentional—not inherited—features. Educators, community members, and families should co-create these values and desired outcomes.

They share a set of agreements, often co-created, designed to create coherence around a few animating ideas. Strategies, structures, schedules, systems, and even spaces are aligned with goals. Everything works together for teachers and learners around a few key priorities. When that priority is difference making, the key feature is big blocks of time and support for extended community-connected work.

A few innovative schools such as Purdue Polytechnic (below) and One Stone organize school primarily around community-connected projects rather than subject-based courses although they do have scheduled skill-building sessions. Difference making is at the heart of the schedule and structure, not an afterthought or extra.

Organizing School Around World Changing Projects

Students at Purdue Polytechnic High School work on big challenges introduced by industry partners (T. Vander Ark, 2019, May 29). For example, Eskenazi Health asked students, "How might we help deliver products or services to help all members of our community to lead a healthier life?" Big questions that might be explored in a related project include cellular structure, heritability, healthy lifestyles, data analysis and statistics, market structures and business models.

Each student schedule is a unique list of projects and dojos—workshops for content acquisition and application. Students have a personal learning coach and an advisory group of 15 to 17 students with whom they start and end their days. The Poly gradebook is a list of "I can" statements. Students progress as they demonstrate mastery through classwork, project demonstrations, or outside activities.

Purdue Polytechnic has three campuses and plans to open another half a dozen Purdue University–connected STEM schools in Indiana.

Difference making can be incorporated into unique aspects of distinctive learning models. These have been referred to as signature learning experiences. They are required or encouraged experiences aimed at meeting a school's priority learning goals. Frequently used examples are senior projects, capstone experiences, service learning requirements, work-based learning, and travel-based learning (T. Vander Ark, 2019, September 10).

Boston Day and Evening Academy re-engages off-track students by providing opportunities to contribute and connect before anything else. They use a competency-based approach to meet students where they are and provide meaningful learning experiences to help them master useful skills, knowledge, and dispositions. Each floor of the three-story building has a student support office with counselors that are constantly engaging with students and providing social and emotional support, as well as connections to community-based resources as needed.

Students at Boston Day and Evening engage in a capstone project that aligns with their goals and interests and often how they want to make a difference. Many students choose to work on a project that directly tackles an immediate issue in their community or their own lives, including topics such as homelessness, food deserts, and crime. Students develop an essential question that focuses their investigation. Capstones include multiple real-world learning experiences including internships or interviews. Products include a cited research paper and a formal presentation. The goal of the project is to prepare students to become resourceful, independent investigators and problem solvers in the world.

Capstone projects like those at Design Tech (discussed in Chapter 3) and Boston Day and Evening are a useful way to build meaningful application into a high school education. Another approach is an optional regional half-day program like Iowa BIG that supports student-selected community-connected projects.

Making a BIG Difference: Unleashing Talent, Inspiring Innovators

Iowa BIG in Cedar Rapids, Iowa, helps students lead their own learning journey while they discover their gifts, talents, and interests. Two school districts helped launch the part-time high school program in 2013 after community conversations prioritized student passions, projects, and community connections. Two more districts have joined BIG. With the second location, BIG serves 250 students.

BIG exists to assist students in developing their agency, efficacy, and passions while gaining valuable real-world and academic skills so they can succeed in a world of rapid and constant change. Most students attend BIG for half of the school day. They sign up for courses, but they turn into interdisciplinary projects that help young people discover their gifts and interests and learn about things they care about.

Two staff members work with community partners to identify projects. Students can choose from this pool of opportunities, or opt to launch their own projects. Teachers help students pack project plans with valuable learning. For important lessons that are not incorporated into projects, teachers hold weekly small-group seminars.

More than just high school credit, students leave BIG with projects accomplished, problems solved, and products in portfolios that share the capabilities they have developed.

Every Friday morning, Quest Early College High School students engage in community service. Learners in the north Houston suburb do about 400 hours of service often including an internship. Service Learning Coordinator Jim Nerad recruits student leaders who help him identify service opportunities that meet authentic needs and empower students to make a positive difference in their local, national, and global communities. Seniors say their service learning experience helped them mature and gain confidence in work and service settings. Teachers at Quest use Friday mornings for professional learning and reviewing student progress.

Community-Connected Contribution

Students at iLEAD Agua Dulce, a K–8 school in north Los Angeles County, use project-based learning to create meaningful change in their community. In 2018, second graders learned about branches of government. They explored the question "How can we implement, follow, or change rules to improve our school and community?" In addition to topics such as longer recess, some of the 8-year-olds wanted to make the road in front of their school safer. They wrote letters to and met with local and state government officials to advocate for speed bumps in the road. The principal said, "We know when given the opportunities, THEY CAN make a difference" ("2nd Graders Creating Change," 2019).

The iLEAD network has schools from Hawaii to Ohio. The acronym spells out network priorities: international (world languages and global competence), leadership, entrepreneurship, artistic expression, and design thinking. "We are a people of purpose," states the iLEAD mission. "We are a caring culture that values community, which contributes to a better society" ("iLEAD Agua Dulce," n.d.)

iLEAD students have opportunities to work on large public projects. Aerospace projects have included Genes in Space, Science Accelerator, unmanned aerial vehicle Design & Flight Training, Dreamup to Space and the Soaring Aeronautics Glider. Students work with groups such as NASA and collaborate with students in other countries.

iLEAD learning spaces are strategically designed to support specific experiences from large group presentations, to seminars, to project teams and individual workspaces. Design studios, makerspace, and immersive learning labs match technology with the driving question (Thornburg, 2013).

Projects at iLEAD include a public product and a presentation of learning to peers, facilitators (teachers), family, and community members. Each year is concluded with a Showcase of Learning where learners and facilitators present reflections on what they have learned and how that has shaped goals and pursuits for the following year.

Empower Generations is an iLEAD program for pregnant and parenting teens. It keeps them in school by providing a customized learning experience that is relevant, meaningful, and supportive. With childcare and wellness programs, iLEAD creates an environment and culture that allows students to take control of their own learning and lives (Niehoff, 2020). It allows them to focus their contribution on creating the best possible conditions for their children.

A School Embedded in the Community

A century-old million-square-foot Sears store and distribution center in the heart of Memphis was renovated beginning in 2015. The Crosstown Concourse is now a vertical urban village including residences, health and recreation organizations, arts and culture facilities, a university, two foundations, retail stores, and restaurants. Opened in 2018 on two floors of the Concourse, Crosstown High engages learners in real-world challenges with community partners and beyond.

The Crosstown High day includes team-taught interdisciplinary project blocks, relationship-building with their advisory group, and personalized learning pursuits. In its location, outreach, enrollment, culture and structure, Crosstown is diverse by design—an important development in Memphis, where neighborhoods and schools are often segregated.

Focused on community contribution, the purpose of Crosstown High is "to prepare students to understand and pursue solutions to the challenges faced by our city and world, and to give students the confidence to be agents of positive change now and in the future."

Students frequently engage in community-connected projects. The ninth-grade team developed a place-based English and AP Geography unit called Project 901 (the local area code) that asked: "What challenges exist in Memphis neighborhoods and how can we design or adapt solutions to address them?" Students toured under-resourced neighborhoods and identified problems. Each student selected a challenge and used design thinking to identify potential solutions to problems such as urban blight and homlessness. They researched and wrote up proposals and benefited from individual feedback at each project milestone.

Introducing young people to their community and exploring the ecology, economy, and culture is what Teton Science Schools (featured below) call place-based education, "integrating learning and community to increase engagement, outcomes, and community impact."

It's what impact entrepreneur CEO Laurie Lane-Zucker (2016) calls "the pedagogy of community, the reintegration of the individual into her homeground and the restoration of the essential links between a person and her place" (para. 8).

Thousands of people visit High Tech High in San Diego every year seeking the secrets to engaging youth in high-quality project-based learning. Founder Larry Rosenstock instructs them to "use the community as text, it's the best and simplest way to get started" (Liebtag, 2019).

Connecting projects to community, delving into authentic problems, and encouraging public products develops an ethic of contribution. It creates a place where "every child and every adult has agency," said Rosenstock. It creates the magical opportunity for learners to make something that wasn't there before.

Restoring Coastal Wetlands in New Orleans

New Harmony High engages students "as change agents in a mission and a movement aimed at addressing the outcomes of coastal restoration that will dramatically shape their future, the lives of their children, and their children's children" (XQ Institute 2019b).

The vision, as the name suggests, is to encourage students to work to find new harmonies and sustainable futures in coastal communities. Each student has the opportunity to create a project of their own design through an internship with a mentor. Graduates will practice resilience and understand ecology—the interconnectedness of people, land, air, and water.

Graduates will be prepared for college, career, and beyond, knowing they have already made a significant impact.

The school opened in Orleans Parish in 2018 with 45 ninth graders and will grow to about 360 students at full enrollment. One first-year example of difference making is New Harmony students studying the quality and quantity of oysters and their habitat in partnership with the Tulane University Biodiversity Research Institute and the National Wildlife Federation. Experts from both groups supported student investigations with local communities of mostly Cambodian and Vietnamese immigrant families (XQ Institute, 2019b).

The Place Network, sponsored by Teton Science Schools (below), makes the case for connecting with place based on four factors: 1) the current model of secondary schools isn't working for most students; 2) most youth are not connecting with local places and in rural areas, and that often means they leave; 3) communities need involvement and engagement to thrive, and learning networks can expand opportunity from school to entire communities; and 4) local and global challenges need innovative solutions.

The Power of Place: Solving Local and Global Challenges

Daily students at Teton Science Schools (TSS) in Jackson, Wyoming, explore environmental issues that threaten Grand Teton National Park and other ecosystems around the world. They share the power of place with thousands of students from around the country every year. Full-time and visitor students benefit from powerful experiences based on six design principles:

- **Local to global context:** Local learning serves as a model for understanding the world around us.

- **Learner-centered:** Learning is personally relevant to each student.

- **Inquiry-based:** Learning is grounded in observing, asking relevant questions, making predictions, and collecting data.

- **Design thinking:** Creative problem-solving is approached systematically.

- **Community as classroom:** Community experts, experiences, and places are part of the expanded definition of a classroom.

- **Interdisciplinary approach:** The curriculum matches the real world where traditional subject areas are taught through integrated, and frequently, project-based approaches.

TSS is helping rural communities throughout the country reimagine their rural futures through the Place Network, an affiliation of small rural schools that "exist to provide an equal opportunity for all learners to make a difference in the world" ("School Network," n.d.).

Place Network partner school students study the economic, cultural, and ecological aspects of place. Projects in 2019 included a tiny home built by eight graders to raise money for a playground and bring awareness to the local housing crisis, designing beehives to improve the health of local ecosystems, and projects on land regenerations, fighting wildfires, and watershed erosion. ("6 Place-Based Projects to Inspire You in the New School Year," 2019).

Difference Making With an Equity Commitment

At Boston Day and Evening Academy, college and career readiness progresses through three phases: Hook, Commit, and Launch. Hook features career exploration including a paid internship to explore job cluster requirements and build basic career readiness skills. In the second phase, students commit to a postsecondary plan and gain additional job-related experience. The individualized Launch phase includes college credit and or job training. The comprehensive approach ensures that all students are on a meaningful postsecondary pathway and that the capstone experience (discussed above) is fully integrated into school and work experiences.

A commitment to equity in difference making requires academic and social scaffolding—a systematic approach to tailoring supports that allow

Urban Seed to Table Changes Eating Habits—and Lives

"Empowering learners by awakening their curiosity and passion to transform themselves and the world." That's the mission at Odyssey STEM Academy in Paramount, a small city and school district just east of Compton in southern Los Angeles County.

With a lot of community input, the school was founded in 2018 by Keith Nuthall and Becky Perez in partnership with Big Picture Learning to demonstrate the potential of compelling community-connected learning in an urban school district. Community conversations led to a set of design principles for the new school: equity, learner-centric, authentic work, learning beyond classroom walls, and family engagement. The Seed to Table program led by Paul Hudak exemplifies these principles. Odyssey students plan, plant, tend to, study, harvest, cook, and share the bounty of a great garden program.

Hudak works with all 140 tenth graders teaching them about environmental sustainability and climate change. "We talk about our roles as humans making solutions and what we can do; we talk about where we have come from and where we are headed," said Hudak.

The once hardscrabble back of the school property now has a 25-by-70 foot greenhouse that serves as a lab and production space. Waste from the tilapia fish fertilizes the aquaponic garden. Students built and decorated thirty raised beds that have over 100 different varieties of herbs, vegetables, and flowers. Students are choosing what to grow; they measure soil composition and develop plans for natural fertilization. A schoolwide composting program supports the garden. Signaling real student ownership, volunteers come in during holiday breaks to tend to the gardens.

Odyssey scholars learn to cook what they grow. When they realized there would be a surplus, several students developed a relationship with Food Finders, a program that sources healthy foods to give to those in need, and organized and scheduled regular deliveries (T. Vander Ark, 2020, January 17).

each child to do their best work. At Boston Day and Evening, it's three phases of support that prepare them for increasingly independent and external work. At Odyssey (featured above) it starts with a community that celebrates the uniqueness of each individual and a commitment that there will be equitable access to programs and opportunities for all. The intentionally diverse school has developed a culture that values achievement as well as trust, care, and respect.

During the last two decades of standards-based reforms, improving test scores became the purpose of schooling in America. It started with a well-intentioned bipartisan commitment to equity but it had the unintended consequence of driving out community connections, art, creativity, and design; it made the work smaller rather than larger; it made the scope narrower instead of broader; it made school a boring rat race toward artificial measures of grade level proficiency.

Charles Fadel, Center for Curriculum Redesign, argues the curriculum should be "flipped so that students spend more time focused on transfer and expertise via concepts rather than on learning content that can now be easily accessed and manipulated" (Vander Ark, 2019, April 1).

Schools profiled in this chapter are shifting from just-in-case learning to learning with cause. Rather than focus on a formula one might need in 15

Connecting Oakland Youth to Meaningful Learning

At Latitude High in Oakland's Fruitvale neighborhood, students participate in extended learning opportunities including studios, internships, and student-designed businesses. In addition to traditional classes, students spend much of their school time in the community: volunteering for local nonprofits, interning at local businesses, meeting with mentors, interviewing local experts and professionals for class projects, and learning about the city around them. Students visit over ten workplaces every year to ignite their career interests and to collaborate with professionals on real-world projects.

Opened in 2018, Latitude will serve 360 students at full enrollment. The goal is for students to leave with "the agency to navigate the complex world" and competencies that equip graduates to be "powerful problem-solvers, communicators, and changemakers."

"We want our students to have a strong sense of agency, a clear sense of where they're going in the future," said founding principal Lillian Hsu. "We want them to have an integrated sense of their own identities. What are they passionate about? What's the impact that they want to have on the world? And we want to make sure they have the academic and social-emotional skills to make those goals happen." (XQ Institute, 2019a).

years, they engage young people in making a contribution where they are. Instead of school as intervention, it's an invitation to contribute. Instead of learning stuff you might need in the future, it's about being fully present in a place and finding ways to leave it better. These schools build agency, collaboration, and creativity while helping learners experience success as they contribute to their community.

It's ironic that a shift away from a focus on preparation (take Algebra 1 because you need it for Algebra 2, which you might need to go to college which you might need to get a job) to a focus on difference making is the best possible form of preparation for the innovation economy. A portfolio of work that demonstrates expanding contribution to causes that matter—to a young person and their community—is far more valuable to most colleges and employers than a list of courses passed. And, because the economy is quickly becoming one where you create a job rather than get a job, helping young people develop an entrepreneurial mindset is the greatest gift we can give them.

What if, instead of a list of required courses, high school was organized around the opportunity to contribute? Jeff Fray sees it as a "big bet for the future: human motivation for meaningful connection and contribution that will hold civic society together."

Educators as Difference Makers

Schools are where students go to learn. They are also a workplace. For students to embrace rigor and intrinsic motivation, it must be modeled by the adults in the workplace. Consider an educator's work environment where:

- Teachers participate in a rigorous improvement process that continually challenges and enhances their mastery of their craft;

- Teachers can make collective decisions about how to teach and collectively decide about what constitutes excellence; and

- Teachers have a shared purpose of making their building one where every child is known, cared for, achieving, and intrinsically motivated.

This is an environment where teachers have ownership and mastery (Bjerede, 2015). It also is important for educators to experience being difference makers outside of serving their students and see themselves as change agents in the broader community.

Ashoka and the LEGO Foundation in their report *Entrepreneurial Patterns for the Future of Learning* encourage "teachers and other adults to not just implement the latest policies and programs, but to be empowered as changemakers: formulating their own solutions, taking action to make them a reality, and quickly adjusting and iterating along the way" (Issuu, 2014). Ashoka offers advice to changemakers who might not know yet how they want to contribute and a map of more than 20,000 changemaker projects from around the world.

Thousands of educators and community members have come together to rally behind teaching toward the Sustainable Development Goals and to provide students more learning experiences focused on service and making a difference (Teach SDGs, n.d.). The global movement includes SDG Ambassadors who lead the charge and engage weekly on social media (#TeachSDGs).

Sharon Davison, elementary school teacher in Vermont and one of the Teach SDG Ambassadors, engages kindergartners in creating "action oriented solutions for problems that can be solved with care and awareness" ("Service Learning," n.d.). She believes "learning through the Global Goals gives great purpose and a strong sense of responsibility to be a part of a solution for problems that impact us all" ("Teaching Through the SDGs," n.d.). Her students complete projects locally to help their immediate environment and connect with other students around the world to understand their pressing issues and challenges (Davison, 2016).

The National Education Association Foundation Global Fellowship provides learning experiences and international field trips for teachers such as Sharon Davison to learn about incorporating global issues into teaching (NEA Foundation, n.d.). Educators work in a cohort to work on a collaborative global project.

Micro-credentials are small units of learning that allow teachers a personalized way to develop, demonstrate, and be recognized for new skills. A growing number support teachers as leaders in difference making. National Geographic Society and Digital Promise created a stack of four micro-credentials to support teachers in service learning ("Service Learning Micro-Credentials," n.d.). National Geographic offers online courses for educators in Teaching Climate Change, Geo-Inquiry, and Service Learning (National Geographic, n.d.).

Community-connected projects can help educators as well as students make a difference in the community. In an effort to reinvigorate Bowie High, a school on the Mexico border just east of downtown El Paso, the school district worked with New Tech Network to develop a project-based school.

Local resident and community artist Maurico Olague found team-teaching a unique art and biology mash-up was invigorating. He designed a project with students to paint murals locally and help beautify the city (Liebtag, 2017, May 31).

When secondary teachers feel empowered and supported as difference makers, they create extraordinary opportunities for youth to connect with local and global challenges and find ways to begin making their unique contributions. The same is true in college. The next chapter features promising developments in educating for contribution in higher education.

CHAPTER
NINE

Colleges for Contribution

No amount of emphasis on narrow specialized courses will produce the innovators we need.

—Richard Miller, President, Olin College

Jemar Lee struggled in high school in Cedar Rapids. "My sophomore journey through the traditional education systems was very rough and rocky," said Lee. "Without purpose and mission, I felt trapped." After a suspension, his principal told Lee about Iowa BIG (introduced in Chapter 8). Within days of enrolling he realized the interest-based program was what he wanted: "I wanted ownership, I didn't want to be lectured, I didn't want to be confined by four walls and bells" (Getting Smart, 2019, February, 20).

He knew he wanted to design spaces. His advisor asked him to design a new space for Iowa BIG. After a bit of floundering on where to start, he excelled as he engaged the community in design options, investigated makerspaces, researched the psychology of learning, and worked with Iowa State Design Lab. Much to his surprise, his design was accepted. "At the age of 16, I was getting a chance to do something I love and impacting my community," said Jemar.

Before attending Morningside College in Sioux City, Lee spent a year serving as an intern with Alliant Energy proposing alternative uses of the piers left from utility bridges swept away in the big 2008 Cedar River flood. Today, the outlook deck on a pedestrian bridge is evidence of a productive internship.

At Morningside, Jemar has been able to construct a learning pathway that combines business administration and public policy with a focus on community planning. Through Project Siouxland, students such as Jamar earn college credits while they work on community problems. Lee especially appreciates the opportunity to build "21st century skills: communication, teamwork, creativity, critical thinking, how to network and how to solve real-world issues" (Siouxland News, 2019).

"Projects are the class, Siouxland is the classroom," at Morningside. It is "all about taking what you learn and immediately putting it into action in the real world. Your project allows you to make a difference in the community while learning by doing. You are in the driver's seat of your education, gaining relevant skills and experience that future employers will love" (Morningside, n.d.).

Jemar Lee has experienced success in serving his community in high school and college. He is a confident, capable changemaker and project manager. Unfortunately, the rich community-connected impact he is experiencing in college is rare.

In this chapter, we discuss

- The crisis of confidence in higher education
- The case for a focus on contribution in high education and examples of where that is happening including the health professions
- Developments in difference making in engineering and environmental studies
- Other postsecondary programs that put students on a path to being difference makers

The College Identity Crisis

Even before the 2019–2020 coronavirus pandemic, higher education was in crisis. Rising costs and graduate underemployment raised questions about value. The majority of Americans lost confidence in the direction higher education was headed and began actively considering lower-cost alternatives and jobs that provide training (Jaschik, 2018).

After 20 years of well-intentioned advocacy by American foundations, a larger percentage of high school graduates have been going to college but showing up with weak preparation, without a clear sense of purpose, and with little guidance on college fit. Rising costs and declining state support have jacked up tuition bills. College costs an average $25,000 a year at public universities—twice that for private schools (ValuePenguin, 2019). Student debt in America has grown to more than $1.5 trillion. About four in ten learners who attempt an undergraduate degree never finish. Many learners drop out after taking loans—the new widespread worst-case scenario of debt without a degree (National Center, 2019).

While learning has never been more important and everyone needs to keep learning throughout their careers, U.S. college enrollments have been declining for a decade. Part of the problem is demographic: the number of high school graduates peaked in 2013 and will fall in the next decade as a result of lower birth rates. There has also been a decline in the number of international students enrolling in American institutions due, in part, to immigration policy. Declining enrollments also signal a perceived loss in value (as well as low unemployment). Millions of young people in high school see underemployed friends and siblings, some that have accumulated debt and realize that the American Dream—predicated on getting a degree and then a good paying job—no longer works for many.

Higher education is not keeping up with the demands of the new economy. While the 5,300 institutions of higher learning in America vary widely, many ascribe to an obsolete model of disconnected courses that cannot deliver competencies for citizenship and contribution in the innovation economy. Millions of employers that used college degrees as a proxy for readiness have realized that diplomas are a weak signal.

JP Morgan Chase CEO Jamie Dimon said:

> A four-year college degree is not the only path to a well-paying job. This outdated thinking is partially to blame for holding back America's growth and blocking many people's access to opportunity. We must consider more inclusive means of hiring the best and most talented people to meet the needs of our rapidly changing economy. (Murray & Meyer, 2019)

Technology companies such as Amazon and Google have started providing their own courses and certifications to build access and boost quality. Indian tech giant Infosys hired more than 2,000 people in America in 2019, many through community college partnerships. "We hire people with adjacent skills and put them through our training program," said CEO Salil Parekh. Infosys training programs range from six weeks to six months. These kinds of free and debt-free sprints to good first jobs are becoming more widely available pathways to high-wage employment. Employers are also becoming more sophisticated about skill-based hiring—it's a "show what you can do" world.

Enabling Contribution in Health Sciences

People considering careers in health care are usually interested in improving the lives and health of other people. Medical schools and health science programs typically promote an ethic of service. They are competency based in that they result in certification, which usually combines passing a test, and on-the-job observation, but that culminates what are typically traditional degrees full of required courses. They are long, expensive, and often procedural in focus—it's easy to lose a focus on the mission to improve lives.

Every medical school has a course in professionalism and in many institutions integrate the concepts throughout the curriculum although approaches vary between a historical focus on moral virtues such as care and compassion, the observable behaviors and competencies that are the focus on certification, and the emerging focus on identity development in a community of practice (Association of American Medical Colleges, 2017, p. 152).

Like law and engineering, medical certification boards have focused on an outcomes-oriented learning model that is anchored in competencies. That is a beneficial way of promoting best practices but can have the unintended consequence of making preparation static and procedural. A focus on identity formation, on the other hand, is adaptive; development is both individual and collective—"it socializes learners into thinking, feeling, and acting like a physician."

Professionalism isn't a definition or metric, concluded Frederic Hafferty, Professor at the Mayo Clinic; it's the "willingness of a community to engage with itself in an ongoing and reflective search for a soul defined by the core values of selflessness and service." It's the "collective ability to function as a beacon of hope where the relentless pounding of market and bureaucratic forces are continuously and conscientiously opposed by another, socially vital way—of organizing work and valuing agency."

Also at the forefront of medical education is shortage of professionals, especially in rural communities. Recognizing that the staggering $190,000 average debt burden taken on by doctors in training prevented them from remaining in or moving to rural communities, John Raymond, MD, the CEO of the Medical College of Wisconsin (MCW), led an initiative to address the problem in three ways. He and his team created immersive regional medical school campuses in two new locations with rural-serving health systems. Five rural systems worked with MCW to provide clinical rotations and teachers for the regional campuses. And they compressed the training from four to three years to reduce the cost and accelerate entry into the profession (Raymond et al., 2017). It's an example of innovative leadership to help aspiring medical professionals serve the communities they care about.

The Case for Contribution in College

The reasons people aspire to teach in the arts and sciences is a desire to advance global knowledge and research and to improve society as a whole. Many faculties promote contribution, but few institutions have a focused mission and aligned programming that makes it a key outcome for all students.

Making a difference takes big blocks of time and community connections. It may involve travel and resources. Unlike colleges, difference making is inherently interdisciplinary. It almost always involves risk of failure. The effort and outcomes are difficult to assess.

Design Thinking at Grand Valley State University

Grand Valley State University (GVSU) created a Design Thinking Academy to prepare students to use creative problem-solving in "high impact activities that contribute to social, civic, and business innovation."

Academy Director David Coffey selected the Innovators' Compass, a design thinking tool distilled by Ela Ben-Ur in work at IDEO, MIT, and Olin College. It involves five questions:

1. People: Who's involved?
2. Observations: What's happening? Why?
3. Principles: What matters most?
4. Ideas: What ways are there?
5. Experiments: What's a step to try?

Academy students use the Innovators' Compass to work on solutions to campus and community issues. One workshop with the university president invited students to co-design the future of GVSU. Students expressed gratitude for having the opportunity to engage in a creative, collaborative problem-solving activity that allows them to plot the path forward.

After a successful project, students are recognized as Design Thinking Fellows, a signal to potential employers that they are experienced in collaboration, problem-solving, and innovation.

Despite the degree of difficulty, identifying and engaging in real-world problems and delivering value to an external audience is the most valuable work a young person can do. It develops the priority skills of leadership and problem-solving. It allows learners to experience success and build confidence in complex real-world settings. It provides motivation to learn sector knowledge and additional skills.

Creating opportunities for contribution requires a significant commitment from a higher education institution. It starts with clarity of purpose that values impact. It is supported by big blocks of time, sustained advisory relationships, and access to flexible resources.

Colleges *could* be the place this preparation happens and students gain interconnected, interdisciplinary experiences that utilize past skills and project them into having meaningful careers and life. Cases included in this chapter highlight quality implementation of purpose-driven programs and institutions. They have fewer random course catalogs and more impact projects aimed at global goals and supported by skill building.

The University of Difference Making

In *Robot-Proof: Higher Education in the Age of Artificial Intelligence*, Northeastern University President Joseph Aoun said there is an opportunity for higher education to lead the way in helping people retool and redefine themselves in a future made uncertain by technology. Aoun, said the students of the future will need to adapt to this changing world by focusing on what makes them unique as humans and by conceiving and creating ideas that are beyond the capabilities of artificial intelligence and smart machines.

This discipline is an integration of three new literacies—understanding technology, understanding data, and understanding what it means to be human—that together form a curriculum he called humanics. It is at the heart of Northeastern University's strategic plan the concept of lifelong and experiential learning that will liberate students from outdated career models and give them the opportunity to prosper over the course of their lives.

On the opposite coast, Azusa Pacific University (APU) in San Diego invites students to "explore your calling" and "join a community of difference makers" (Azusa Pacific University, n.d.). Highlighted front and center for prospective students are the stories of how current and past students have made a difference in the world and found their calling at APU. All of the students at APU receive some form of financial aid.

Alumnus of APU masters and doctoral programs, Dr. Kaleb Rashad from High Tech High Graduate School shared about his experience, "If empathy is innovation fuel, APU cultivated it within and across communities, seeding the soil for healthy, sustainable and adaptable change" (personal communication, 2019). He has continued to be a difference maker in the world, working to help unleash the potential of thousands of educators and students every year.

World Changers Conduct Impact Projects in Seven Cities

Living in seven cities in four years, each cohort of about 150 undergraduate Minerva students engages in interactive online seminars and conducts impact projects that apply and extend their learning. Each location presents new opportunities to work on a range of social issues with local partners. In their fourth year, students take electives, design their own seminars with faculty support, and complete their own capstone projects.

Sponsored by Keck Graduate Institute at Claremont, Minerva offers a rigorously designed curriculum that develops knowledge and skills in about 100 foundational concepts and habits of success. Students focus on thinking critically and creatively and communicating and interacting effectively. The first class of world changers graduated in May 2019.

Among the first graduating class was Xiaotian Liao. Her capstone project included research on hemophilia she conducted at the Harvard Stem Cell Institute and investigations into methods to improve CRISPR gene editing outcomes. The project built on skills developed in her double majors, natural sciences and computational sciences. Liao now serves as a Research Assistant at Boston Children's Hospital and the Broad Institute.

In the narrowest sense, Minerva is an extraordinary leadership development option for the world's smartest young people. More broadly, it is a reconceptualization of college as an impact engine with interactive skill sprints and location-based projects (Minerva, 2019).

Things are even starting to change at Harvard. Raj Chetty has recast an introduction to economics as an opportunity to use data to solve economic and social problems. Chetty wants to help students think deeper about society and how economics can be at play. Given the pressing issues of our time, in his course he describes economics as "essentially, a kind of applied statistics, an attempt to use quantitative data to answer social questions" (Matthews, 2019). Students use what they learn about economics and data to work on problems "addressing inequality, specifically: in their own neighborhoods, in housing, in education."

Chetty isn't the only professor at Harvard looking to empower students to make a difference. Harvard Business School declares a mission bold and big, focused on making a difference: "We educate leaders who make a difference in the world" (Harvard Business School, n.d.).

The Harvard Graduate School for Education attracts scholars "with a passion to contribute to the world through education." Dean Bridget Long promises, "You will leave here with the knowledge, skills, and relationships that will empower you to make meaningful change in the lives of students of all ages" (2019).

The Danforth Education Leadership program at the University of Washington is another preparation program committed to "equity and excellence for all." Leaders develop core competencies including shaping culture and leading change.

Mia Williams, Principal at Aki Kurose Middle School in Seattle and Danforth graduate, said, "Equity and excellence is a big part of the social justice focus of Danforth, and just being student centered, being in a collaborative, data-driven process and having the different modules that help lead there."

Engineering for Impact

Engineering education programs have traditionally been transactional and computational—focused on first job skills and the traditional rules and calculations made by entry-level professionals. But that is changing fast. Preparation programs around the country are incorporating data analytics and encouraging engineers in training to consider broader impacts of their work.

Dr. Paul Johnson, President of the Colorado School of Mines, explained that in the past, engineering education was preoccupied with assessing individual proficiency in calculations. "In education today, particularly at Mines, we work on open-ended problems, more design challenges, working in groups with the opportunity to work on teams competing in national engineering challenges. You can see a lot more connection between what you're working on and what the impact of that work is on society" (Vander Ark, 2019, June 17).

Engineering Solutions to Better Humanity

At Olin College, "doing good for humanity" is a founding precept. A 20-year-old purpose-built engineering program, Olin trains engineer-innovators to envision and deliver products, services, and systems that transform the way people live on this planet (Olin College, n.d.).

Olin was founded to reimagine undergraduate engineering education. The founding board recognized that traditional education was too narrow, compartmentalized, and focused on solving known problems rather than encouraging learners to find problems worth solving.

From Day 1, Olin engineers are using design thinking to understand the people they are serving, what they value, and where opportunities exist to create value. Students learn how to envision positive change, how to prototype solutions, and also how to realize and deliver that change.

Computer Science professor Amon Millner appreciates how the Olin faculty "blend engineering, entrepreneurial mindset, and an appreciation for the variety of human conditions," into integrated hands-on project-based experiences (T. Vander Ark, 2019, March 20).

The Olin curriculum is based on the idea that engineering starts with people—understanding who we're designing for, what they value, and where opportunities to create value exist—and ends with people—appreciating the social context of our work and making a positive difference in the world. At Olin, students learn how to envision positive change and also how to realize and deliver that change.

Olin College was founded because we believe there is a problem with undergraduate engineering education. The traditional curriculum is too narrow; it teaches students how to solve problems, but not how to find the right problems to solve, or how to get their solutions out of the lab and into the world (Olin College of Engineering, n.d.).

Mines, Olin, and 45 more leading universities are members of the KEEN network. They share a commitment to infusing entrepreneurial mindset in engineering education so that graduate engineers go on to create more personal, economic, and societal value through a lifetime of meaningful work.

Unlike business schools, which often view entrepreneurship as a set of skills specific to starting a business, these engineering schools cultivate an impact-oriented mindset that could be deployed in a big company or social enterprise as well as a startup. KEEN members share a framework focused on design, opportunity, and impact. "Students will identify unexpected opportunities to create extraordinary value and persist through and learn from failure" (Engineering Unleashed, n.d.b).

Terry Obeng-Ampomah served as an entrepreneurial resource to his peers at Arizona State University, another KEEN member, while completing his master's degree in mechanical engineering. As an environmental advocate and researcher at the ASU Biodesign Institute, Terry is working on solutions for direct capture of atmospheric CO_2. He also worked on a water purification project for Puerto Rico after hurricane Maria. Terry wants to be an engineer and an entrepreneur making a positive impact and is an example of a student who has benefited from a program focused on spotting opportunity and delivering impact.

From Extraction to Contribution

For almost 150 years, Colorado School of Mines has been the best college in the world for extracting resources from the earth. It taught prospective engineers to memorize formulas and follow rules. In the last decade, Mines has been transformed into a global leader in education and research to solve the world's challenges related to the earth, energy, and environment.

"The value of engineering in the future isn't how well students do calculation—that aspect of engineering has been replaced by computers," said Mines President Paul Johnson.

"Sustainability is a very important topic that our graduates need to understand," said Johnson. There are now a variety of courses focused on sustainability and lifecycle assessment.

For those in the extractive industry, "Sustainability is not just an environmental issue; it's an economic issue," explained Johnson. "You have to look at yourself as a steward of the earth asking yourself, what was the value of the property before and after I leave?"

Hundreds of Mines students take courses in humanitarian engineering, which brings together engineering and social science professors to transform the ways engineers are taught to think, define, and solve problems with communities. It's part of a new division that is also home to Design@Mines, a sequence of courses that develop creativity and problem-solving skills beginning with Cornerstone, an introduction to engineering, and concluding with Capstone, a senior design project.

There is more active and project-based learning across campus. The shift from content transmission to critical thinking and problem-solving has been supported by a 5-year-old center for teaching and learning.

Engineers in training at the University of Dayton have the opportunity to participate in Engineers in Technical Humanitarian Opportunities of Service Learning (Ethos). The travel and service program is rooted in the belief that "engineers are more capable to serve our world when they experience opportunities that increase their understanding of technology's global linkage with values, culture, society, politics and economics." Over the last 20 years, ETHOS has sent 330 students to 20 different countries, working with 40 project sponsors.

Climate Action

There is accelerating recognition of the impact humans are having on the planet. Young people might be the last generation with a chance to mitigate the damage and the first with opportunities to build adaptations to living on a hot planet. Many young people today are seeking experiences that help them be a part of the solution. A growing number of universities have programs that help young people begin to make their initial contribution to the environment.

The Evergreen State College in Olympia, Washington, was rated by *Washington Monthly* as the top Master's University for promoting social mobility, research, and public service (Thurston Talk, 2019; U.S. News, n.d.).

Evergreen's interdisciplinary master of environmental studies engages learners in the complex work of environmental leadership.

Undergraduates have the opportunity to create unique pathways. They focus not on majors and minors "but on layering disciplines into individual expressions of scholarship and anticipating careers yet to be invested." Pathways include impact projects and evidence collected in portfolios. They evaluate not with traditional grades but with context and explanation. The focus is not tradition but invention.

Building a Future for Everyone

The School for the Future of Innovation in Society (SFIS) is a transdisciplinary unit at leading Arizona State's commitment to linking innovation to public value. It integrates diverse knowledge and perspectives, blends technical and social concerns, and teaches to build "futures we want to inhabit" (ASU, 2017).

The undergraduate Innovations in Society degree teaches students how to think critically about how changes in technology affect society, how to apply "future thinking" to analyze emerging trends and plausible futures, how to compare change forces, and how to facilitate change.

A certificate program supports ASU students who identify a problem and work with peers, mentors, and the community to produce innovations that cultivate a better future for society.

As a master's student, Kayla Kutter studied the energy trilemma: security, equity, and sustainability. She studied the interactions among public and private actors, governments and regulators, economic and social factors, national resources, environmental concerns, and individual behaviors. She now leads sustainable procurement for the University of Colorado.

Sasha Barab (introduced in Chapter 2) teaches in SFIS and is piloting a human development platform that develops skills to unlock potential and connects people through their stories.

College of the Atlantic, located on an island in the middle of a national park in Maine, is a small school with a big vision. Dedicated to "transforming thought into action to make a difference in the world, starting now," each COA learner designs a course of study in human ecology—an exploration of the relationships between humans and their natural, cultural, and built environments. Students work collaboratively on meaningful projects (College of the Atlantic, n.d.).

Chatham University in Pittsburgh is consistently ranked one of the greenest colleges in America. The mission is "to prepare students to build lives of purpose, value, and fulfilling work . . . by preparing graduates to be informed and engaged citizens in their communities; to recognize and respect diversity of culture, identity, and opinion; and to live sustainably."

Chatham's Falk School of Sustainability & Environment is the first academic community in the world built from the ground up for the study of sustainable living, learning, and development. On the 388-acre campus of wooded and agricultural land, Falk students combine environmental research with big data science to contribute to sustainability.

Students on their own accord might take on a challenging problem, one that their specific discipline of study or program area might not connect to at first glance but has real value when they apply the skills they are learning. For example, UVA students made a site to track the COVID-19 outbreak in the spring of 2020 (Samarrai, 2020). The students state, "Skills we develop here set us up to impact the world in tangible ways, like creating this web application that is meant to educate people about the dangers of a life-threatening virus . . . represent my school well as I go out into my career, aiding humanity on a large scale."

Learn and Earn

Cost is the biggest barrier to accessing a meaningful postsecondary education. Financed degrees are not realistic for millions of families and they aren't yielding the return they once may have. Learning and working at the same time is not just more reasonable but also has the potential to provide applied learning experiences when the job and area of study align.

All full-time residential students at Paul Quinn College in Dallas work between 300 and 400 hours each year in order to earn a tuition grant of $5,000 and a cash payment of between $1,000 and $1,500. In addition to covering much of the tuition, the Work Program encourages students to "embrace the ideals of disciplined work, servant leadership, and initiative in preparation for lives of financial freedom, community engagement, and outstanding character." Students at the only urban work college are evaluated on 10 workplace skills and attributes. Quinn operates on a beautiful set of guiding principles: leave places better than you found them, lead from wherever you are, live a life that matters, love something greater than yourself.

The mission of Antioch College in Yellow Springs, Ohio, is to "win victories for humanity." This theme and mission is integrated into all aspects of the college and learner experiences. Students have full-time co-op experiences while at Antioch and create difference-making projects alongside both

Working Adults Complete Degrees and Contribute

Jose Rodriguez grew up in Providence without many options. As a young man, he went to prison for attempted murder. After getting out, he enrolled in a community college but was frustrated with his slow progress. After finding College Unbound, Jose earned an associate's degree in six months. But after getting in a fight, Jose went back to prison. Fortunately, there was a cohort of College Unbound in prison and he was able to continue making progress. Once released, he graduated. Rodriguez is now house manager at a shelter and recruiter for College Unbound. And he's working on a graduate degree.

After 15 years of success advancing a radically student-centered high school model through Big Picture Learning, Dennis Littky created College Unbound to extend the same idea of starting with student interest and constructing a pathway to success to helping first-generation low-income working adults complete a college degree (T. Vander Ark, 2019, April 22).

College Unbound is affordable and accessible with classes offered during times that work for the students' schedules. Across all of their real-world projects, Unbound learners focus on the "Big 10" leadership skills—including advocacy for self and others, intercultural engagement, critical thinking, and creativity—to make a contribution to their place of employment and community.

their classmates and the local community. Real-world experiences are a main component of the Antioch experience. At Antioch, students craft and self-design a major that fits their needs and how they want to contribute. Those who are eligible for a Federal Pell Grant can receive full-tuition scholarships, placement in integrated work programs, and support for job placement after graduation, helping to make higher education valuable and affordable (Lippincott, 2019).

Northeastern University, a leader in experiential education and cooperative learning experiences, focuses on finding gainful, purpose-driven and meaningful employment for every student. The Career Design Team helps students find meaningful experiences and employment while attending Northeastern. While the intent is most focused on career path development, one of the main desired outcomes is that students become active global citizens that are contributing meaningful work (Northeastern University, n.d.).

New Roads to Contribution

Ryan Craig is the most influential investor in emerging postsecondary learning models. In his 2018 book *A New U: Faster + Cheaper Alternatives to College*, he suggests that free (or debt free) sprints to good first jobs will replace a big chunk of higher education. Rather than two years of general education and then a specific major, Craig argues that most people would be better off starting with job-specific training and, once they have climbed a couple rungs on the economic ladder, continue learning in what will frequently be sponsored programs.

There is a growing number of advocates for flipping the college degrees and starting with job certificates to provide immediate value, then following with a flexible, modular, often sponsored approach to additional certificates and degrees.

Our friendly amendment to this trend is a hard sprint to a first contribution. It may be lined up with a specific job, but chances are, difference making opens more doors. After leading a community-connected project, a young person is more employable, more sponsorable, and has more options for expanded impact.

Education as contribution combines academic preparation and real-world impact. It's applied, it's relevant, it's collaborative, it's motivating, and it's productive—for learners and communities. It's the new preparation for the innovation economy and a world of opportunity and challenge.

Conclusion

The climate crisis, the rise of artificial intelligence, and shocks of pandemics underscore our new mutuality. Thriving—maybe even surviving—in the innovation economy and the age of superintelligence after that will require novel solutions and new ways to share.

We're All in This Together

Our new mutuality requires more connectivity, community, and commitment to making a difference in the world. Working together and uplifting communities—especially those who are often overlooked and underserved—require this mutual commitment to the imperative issues of our time and addressing them through collective action.

Every person has unique strengths and interests with enormous potential to contribute. Global platforms and smart tools make it easier than ever to make a difference. Now we have the opportunity to build systems that, rather than disconnecting and discriminating against groups of people, lift people up and enable contribution.

Everyone Has a Big Next Step

Given the extraordinary opportunities and dynamic challenges we face, schools and colleges can be more than skill-building transactions. They can introduce young people to the world and cultivate contribution. They can be learning environments and experiences that help young people develop a sense of purpose and begin making a difference.

Engaging young people in community-connected challenges is not only engaging and motivating, it's the most valuable form of preparation. It can engage youth in surveying the world for problems worth solving. It builds leadership, applies design thinking, and develops an entrepreneurial mindset.

Difference Making: Schools Alive With Possibility

Schools and colleges can be launching pads for difference making. It's time to make learning more meaningful and valuable for young people. Many schools across the country and around the world have already taken on these new priorities and placed difference making the heart of learning.

What if learning experiences were focused on making a difference in the world? What if we invited in the opportunity for young people to take on the biggest challenges of our time? Learners focused on solving issues and making a difference in their local communities and globally are our best hope at getting things right in the future.

We know each and every young person has the potential to be the change agents who make a real difference in our world. Young people have already begun to rise up and feel empowered to make change in their own communities. Solutionaries around the world have been making their voices heard.

The next decade will inevitably bring more challenges and likely more questions than answers, but it also could bring promise and potential for a better future if schools help create the space and support for all learners to make a difference.

How will you make a difference?

Bibliography

2016 Gallup Student Poll: A Snapshot of Results and Findings. (2017). Retrieved from https://news.gallup.com/reports/210995/6.aspx? ays=n#aspnetForm

24 Goals to Save the Planet (+1 In Case We Don't). (2020). Retrieved from https://www.forbes.com/sites/tomvanderark/2020/01/06/24-goals-to-save-the-planet-1-in-case-we-dont/?fbclid=IwAR1b1JZtpljJKDBnTsMF2q0uilchkGvI98XKQjiazxreatg1xwuvHQ_PIBM#13e890953f26

2nd Graders Creating Change. (2019, May 25). Retrieved from https://ileadaguadulce.org/2nd-graders-creating-change/

6 Place-Based Projects to Inspire You in the New School Year. (2019, August 8). Retrieved from https://www.tetonscience.org/6-place-based-projects-to-inspire-you-in-the-new-school-year/

8 Ways Nelson Mandela Changed the World. (2018, July 18). Retrieved from https://www.red.org/reditorial/2018/7/18/8-ways-nelson-mandela-changed-the-world.

Abby Falik on the benefits of global service. (2019). *Getting Smart* [Audio podcast]. Retrieved from https://www.gettingsmart.com/2019/09/podcast-abby-falik-on-the-benefits-of-global-service/

ACT Research. (2016). *College choice report: Class of 2015.* Retrieved from http://www.act.org/content/act/en/research/reports/act-publications/college-choice-report.html

Aglio, J. (2018, July 19). *Montour school district: America's first public school AI program.* Retrieved from https://www.gettingsmart.com/2018/07/coming-this-fall-to-montour-school-district-americas-first-public-school-ai-program/

Aglio, J. (2019, January 23). *An inside look—America's first public school AI program.* Retrieved from https://www.gettingsmart.com/2019/01/an-inside-look-americas-first-public-school-ai-program/

AI4All Extends the Power of Artificial Intelligence to High School Girls. (2018, March 1). Retrieved from https://www.gettingsmart.com/2018/03/ai4all-extends-power-artificial-intelligence-high-school-girls/

Alter, C. (2018, March 22). The school shooting generation has had enough. *Time.*

American Psychological Association. (2018). Retrieved from https://www.apa.org/science/about/psa/2018/06/motivation

Anderson-Minshall, D. (2019, June 3). *Meet the queer kid pushing for a Green New Deal.* Retrieved from https://www.advocate.com/exclusives/2019/6/03/meet-queer-kid-pushing-new-green-deal

Arizona State University. (n.d.a). Retrieved from https://entrepreneurship.engineering.asu.edu/keen-entrepreneurial-catalysts/

Arizona State University. (n.d.b). Retrieved from https://sfis.asu.edu/sites/default/files/2017-18_annual_report-web.pdf

Asia Society. (n.d.). What is global competence? In *Center for Global Education.* Retrieved from https://asiasociety.org/education/what-global-competence

Aspen Institute. (n.d.) *Weave: The social fabric project.* Retrieved from https://www.aspeninstitute.org/programs/weave-the-social-fabric-initiative/

Average Cost of College in America. (n.d.). Retrieved from https://www.valuepenguin.com/student-loans/average-cost-of-college

Azusa Pacific University. (n.d.). *Undergraduate admissions.* (n.d.). Retrieved from https://www.apu.edu/admissions/#undergraduate

B Corps. (2019). *Best for the world: Changemaker list.* Retrieved from https://bcorporation.uk/2019-best-for-the-world-changemaker

Barron, A. (2017, March 23). *Why we use digital badges at Del Lago Academy.* Retrieved from https://www.gettingsmart.com/2017/03/why-we-use-digital-badges-at-del-lago-academy/

Baumeister, R. F. (1991). *Meanings of life.* New York, NY: Guilford Press. Retrieved from https://www.amazon.com/Meanings-Life-Roy-F-Baumeister/dp/0898625319

Bee and the Fox (2019, February 2). *Black History Month: James Baldwin.* Retrieved from https://www.thebeeandthefox.com/blogs/news/black-history-month-james-baldwin

Belli, B. (2020). *National survey: Students' feelings about high school are mostly negative.* Retrieved from https://news.yale.edu/2020/01/30/national-survey-students-feelings-about-high-school-are-mostly-negative

Benefit Mindset. (n.d.). Retrieved from http://www.benefitmindset.com/

The Better Their World Student Project Database. (n.d.). *The Global Future Education and Institute.* Retrieved from http://btwdatabase.org/

Bjerede, M. (2015, August 28). *Students deserve a culture of rigor and intrinsic motivation.* Retrieved from https://www.gettingsmart.com/2015/08/students-deserve-a-culture-of-rigor-and-intrinsic-motivation/

Bjerede, M. (2018, May 18). *What counts as student agency?* Retrieved from https://www.gettingsmart.com/2018/05/what-counts-as-student-agency/

BlackSpace. (n.d.). About. Retrieved from http://theblackspace.org/about/

Boggs, G. L., Kurashige, S., Glover, D., & Wallerstein, I. M. (2012). The Next American revolution: Sustainable activism for the twenty-first century. Berkeley, CA: University of California Press.

Boggs Center. (n.d.). Retrieved from http://boggscenter.org/

Boggs School. (n.d.). Mission & Core Ideology. Retrieved from http://www.boggsschool.org/mission-core-ideology

Bridgeland, J. M., DiIulio, J. J., & Morison, K. B. (2006). The silent epidemic perspectives of high school dropouts. *Civil Enterprises.*

Buchanan, A., & Kern, M. L. (2017). The benefit mindset: The psychology of contribution and everyday leadership. *International Journal of Wellbeing, 7*(1), 1–11. Retrieved from https://internationaljournalofwellbeing.org/index.php/ijow/article/view/538/593

Bull City Schools. (2019, June 14). *DPS Foundation Grant Highlight—Pauli Murray mural at Hillside* [Video]. *YouTube.* Retrieved from https://youtube/unF_ndzmUMU

Byron Sanders on closing the opportunity gap in Dallas. (2020, April 15). *Getting Smart* {Audio podcast]. Retrieved from https://www.gettingsmart.com/2020/04/podcast-byron-sanders-on-closing-the-opportunity-gap-in-dallas/

Cabrera, J. (2017, February 17). *Embracing the border economy.* Retrieved from https://www.gettingsmart.com/2017/02/embracing-border-economy/

Clifford, C. (2019, July 17). *Jeff Bezos: I spend my billions on space because we're destroying Earth.* Retrieved from https://www.cnbc.com/2019/07/17/why-jeff-bezos-spends-billions-on-space-technology.html

College of the Atlantic. (n.d.). *About COA*. Retrieved from https://www.coa.edu/about/

Cone Communications. (2016). *2016 Cone communications millennial employee engagement study*. Boston, MA: Cone.

Consortium for Public Education. (n.d.). *The Future Is mine*. Retrieved from https://www.theconsortiumforpubliceducation.org/what-we-do/the-future-is-mine/

Craig, R. (2019, July 28). *Last-mile training and the future of work in an expanding gig economy*. Retrieved from https://techcrunch.com/2019/07/28/last-mile-training-and-the-future-of-work-in-an-expanding-gig-economy/

Curtin, S. C., & Heron, M. (2019). *Death rates due to suicide and homicide among persons aged 10–24: United States, 2000–2017*. Retrieved from https://www.cdc.gov/nchs/data/databriefs/db352-h.pdf

Damon, W. (2010). *The path to purpose: How young people find their calling in life*. New York, NY: Free Press.

Davison, S. E. (2016, August 13). *GlobalEd connectivity in the kindergarten classroom*. Retrieved from https://www.gettingsmart.com/2016/08/globaled-connectivity-in-the-kindergarten-classroom/

Del Lago Academy Campus of Applied Science. (n.d.a). Retrieved from https://www.dellagoacademy.org/apps/pages/missionstatement

Del Lago Academy Campus of Applied Science. (n.d.b). Retrieved from https://www.dellagoacademy.org/apps/pages/principalsmessage

Deloitte. (2019). The Deloitte global millennial survey 2019.

Design for Change i CAN marketplace. (n.d.). *Design for Change*. Retrieved from https://icanmarketplace.dfcworld.com/

Design for Change research. (n.d.). *Design for Change*. Retrieved from https://www.dfcworld.com/SITE/Research

Design for Change. (n.d.). Retrieved from https://www.dfcworld.com/SITE

Don Wettrick on teaching entrepreneurship. (2019, August 14). *Getting Smart* [Audio podcast]. Retrieved from https://www.gettingsmart.com/2019/08/podcast-don-wettrick-on-teaching-entrepreneurship/

Doyle. (2019, December 21). *A solstice dawn prayer*. Retrieved from https://www.science-teacher.net/2019/12/21/a-solstice-dawn-prayer/

Dubner, S. J. (2020, January 1). The zero-minute workout (Ep. 383 Rebroadcast) [Audio podcast]. Freakonomics. Retrieved from http://freakonomics.com/podcast/exercise-rebroadcast/

Duffin, E. (2019, December 11). *Number of business establishments less than 1 year old in the United States, March 1994 to March 2019*. Retrieved from https://www.statista.com/statistics/235494/new-entrepreneurial-businesses-in-the-us/

EL Education. (n.d.). Retrieved from https://eleducation.org/resources/agency

Engineering Unleashed. (n.d.a). About Us. Retrieved from https://engineeringunleashed.com/about.aspx

Engineering Unleashed. (n.d.b). Framework. https://engineeringunleashed.com/framework

Engle, J. (2019, April 24). What do you think are the beliefs and values that define American culture? *The New York Times*. Retrieved from https://www.nytimes.com/2019/04/24/learning/what-do-you-think-are-the-beliefs-and-values-that-define-american-culture.html

Eric Williams on empowering students to make a contribution. (2019, November 5). *Getting Smart* [Audio podcast]. Retrieved from https://www.gettingsmart.com/2019/11/podcast-eric-williams-on-empowering-students-to-make-a-contribution/

Eskreis-Winkler, L., Milkman, K. L., Gromet, D. M., & Duckworth, A. L. (2019). A large-scale field experiment shows giving advice improves academic outcomes for the advisor. *Proceedings of the National Academy of Sciences, 116*(30), 14808–14810. Retrieved from https://doi.org/10.1073/pnas.1908779116.

Evergreen State College. (n.d.) Academics. Retrieved from https://evergreen.edu/academics

Fink, L. (2019). *Larry Fink's letter to CEOs*. Retrieved from https://www.blackrock.com/corporate/investor-relations/larry-fink-ceo-letter

Forbes. (2019). *Images of Typhoon Hagibis overwhelming Japan are stunning*. Retrieved from https://www.forbes.com/sites/ericmack/2019/10/13/images-of-typhoon-hagibis-overwhelming-japan-are-stunning/#6bb636c73d73

Future of Humanity Institute. (n.d.). About FHI. Retrieved from https://www.fhi.ox.ac.uk/about-fhi/#1490202129495-2bef7859-ad1c

Future of Life Institute. (n.d.a). *Benefits & risks of biotechnology*. (n.d.). Retrieved from https://futureoflife.org/background/benefits-risks-biotechnology/

Future of Life Institute. (n.d.b). *The risk of nuclear weapons*. Retrieved from https://futureoflife.org/background/the-risk-of-nuclear-weapons

Gates, M. (2019). The moment of lift: How empowering women changes the world. *CELA*.

Geiger, A. W., & Davis, L. (2019). A growing number of American teenagers—particularly girls—are facing depression. *Pew Research Center*. Retrieved from https://www.pewresearch.org/fact-tank/2019/07/12/a-growing-number-of-american-teenagers-particularly-girls-are-facing-depression/

Getting Smart. (2016). *Community conversations shape portrait of a graduate*. Retrieved from https://www.gettingsmart.com/2016/01/community-conversations-shape-portrait-graduate/

Getting Smart. (2017). *Embracing the border economy*. Retrieved from https://www.gettingsmart.com/2017/02/embracing-border-economy/

Getting Smart. (2018, January 17). *High tech exec advocates for high agency learning*. Retrieved from https://www.gettingsmart.com/2018/01/high-tech-exec-advocates-for-high-agency-learning/

Getting Smart. (2018, September 13). *Why youth need social capital and how schools can help*. Retrieved from https://www.gettingsmart.com/2018/09/why-youth-need-social-capital-and-how-schools-can-help/

Getting Smart. (2019a). *Engineering good in the world*. Retrieved from https://www.gettingsmart.com/2019/05/engineering-good-in-the-world/

Getting Smart. (2019b). *Making the city the text at High Tech High*. Retrieved from https://www.gettingsmart.com/2019/01/making-the-city-the-text-at-high-tech-high-pod-repost/

Getting Smart. (2019c). *Purdue Poly: Driven by equity, solving community challenges*. Retrieved from https://www.gettingsmart.com/2019/05/purdue-poly-driven-by-equity-solving-community-challenges/

Getting Smart. (2019, February 20). *Learner-Centered Iowa BIG Propels Jemar Lee*. Retrieved from https://www.gettingsmart.com/2019/02/learner-centered-iowa-big-propels-jemar-lee/

Getting Smart. (2020, January 2). *Building transferable skills: Design Tech High at Oracle Campus*. Retrieved from https://www.gettingsmart.com/2018/04/building-transferable-skills-design-tech-high-at-oracle-campus/

Global Citizen. (n.d.) *2019 Global Citizen Prize: Cisco Youth Leadership Award will honor one extraordinary global citizen—Will it be you?* Retrieved from https://www.globalcitizen .org/en/content/Global-Citizen-Prize-Cisco-Youth-Leadership-2019/

Global Dignity. (2017, October 18). *Global Dignity Day 2011 | Archbishop Desmond Tutu* [Video]. YouTube. Retrieved from https://youtu.be/V8nG2kuAseM

The Global Goals. (n.d.). Retrieved from https://www.globalgoals.org/

Global Oneness Project. (n.d.) *Document your place on the planet*. Retrieved from https://www .globalonenessproject.org/student-projects/document-your-place-planet-remember-earth

Global Shapers Community. (n.d.). *Values*. Retrieved from https://www.globalshapers.org/ impact/themes/values

Godin, S. (2012). *Stop stealing dreams: (What is school for?)*.

Godin, S. (2018a). *Hilbert's list*. Retrieved from https://seths.blog/2018/12/hilberts-list/

Godin, S. (2018b). *This is marketing: You can't be seen until you learn to see*. London, *England: Portfolio Penguin*.

Godin, S. (2020, January 1). *A box of infinity*. Retrieved from https://seths.blog/2020/01/ a-box-of-infinity/

Graham, R. (2018, March). *The global state of the art in engineering education*. Retrieved from http://neet.mit.edu/wp-content/uploads/2018/03/MIT_NEET_GlobalState EngineeringEducation2018.pdf

Green Bronx Machine. (n.d.). About. Retrieved from https://greenbronxmachine.org/about/

Hansen, U. J. (2019, December 11). *Hansen: Transforming our schools so they engage students and empower them with a sense of purpose*. Retrieved from https://www.the74million.org/ article/hansen-transforming-our-schools-so-they-engage-students-and-empower-them-with-a-sense-of-purpose/

Harvard Business School. (n.d.). *Our mission*. (n.d.). Retrieved from https://www.hbs.edu/ about/Pages/mission.aspx

Harvard Graduate School of Education. (2020). Retrieved from https://www.gse.harvard.edu/ about/dean/welcome

Haupt, A. (2010, November). Volunteering does a body good. *U.S. News & World Report, 72.*

Hellams, R. (2019). *Del Lago Academy student handbook*. Retrieved from https://wpmediaeuhsd .blob.core.windows.net/wp-media/2017/12/DLA_Handbook_Final_Draft_2017-2018.pdf

Hewlett Foundation. (2014). *Deeper learning for every student every day*. Retrieved from https:// hewlett.org/wp-content/uploads/2016/08/Deeper%20Learning%20for%20Every%20 Student%20EVery%20Day_GETTING%20SMART_1.2014.pdf

Hillman, J. (2017). *The soul's code: In search of character and calling*. New York, NY: Ballantine Books.

hooks, b. (2001). *All about love: New vision*. Retrieved from http://wtf.tw/ref/hooks.pdf

hooks, b. (2009). *Belonging: A culture of place*. Abingdon, England: Routledge.

hooks, b. (2018). *All about love: New visions*. New York, NY: William Morrow.

Hugo Marquez. (2016, February 27). *Unsung hero project* [Video]. *YouTube*. Retrieved from https://youtu.be/S7iRLjXH27w

IES NCES National Center for Education Statistics. (2020). Retrieved from https://nces
.ed.gov/programs/coe/indicator_ctr.asp

iLEAD Agua Dulce. (n.d.). Retrieved from https://ileadaguadulce.org/

Inside Higher Ed. (2018). *Falling confidence in higher ed.* (2018). Retrieved from https://www
.insidehighered.com/news/2018/10/09/gallup-survey-finds-falling-confidence-higher-education

International Labour Organization. (n.d.). *Helping the gig economy work better for gig workers.*
Retrieved from https://www.ilo.org/washington/WCMS_642303/lang--en/index.htm

Issuu. (2014, May 14). *Social innovation mapping: Entrepreneurial patterns for the future of
learning.* Retrieved from https://issuu.com/ashokachangemakers/docs/social-innovation-
mapping-entrepren/8

Jaschik, S. (2018). *Falling Confidence in Higher Ed.* Retrieved from https://www. Insidehighered
.com/news/2018/10/09/gallup-survey-finds-falling-confidence-higher-education

Joseph Campbell Foundation. (2019, April 28). *Follow your bliss.* Retrieved from https://www
.jcf.org/about-joseph-campbell/follow-your-bliss/

Keegan, M. (2019, December 2). *Big Brother is watching: Chinese city with 2.6m cameras is world's
most heavily surveilled.* Retrieved from https://www.theguardian.com/cities/2019/dec/02/
big-brother-is-watching-chinese-city-with-26m-cameras-is-worlds-most-heavily-surveilled

Kendi, I. (2017). *Explaining how to be an "antiracist," Ibram X. Kendi rattles conventional wisdom.*
Retrieved from https://www.bates.edu/news/2017/10/26/kendi/

Khullar, D. (2018, January 1). Finding purpose for a good life. But also a healthy one. *The
New York Times.* Retrieved from https://www.nytimes.com/2018/01/01/upshot/finding-
purpose-for-a-good-life-but-also-a-healthy-one.html

KidsRights Changemakers. (2019). *Desmond Tutu announces the winners of the International
Children's Peace Prize 2019.* Retrieved from https://www.thekidsrightschangemakers.org/en/
news/desmond-tutu-announces-the-winners-of-the-international-childrens-peace-prize-20

KidsRights Changemakers. (n.d.) *Get started.* Retrieved from https://www.thekidsrights
changemakers.org/en/program

Kincaid, J. (2000). *A small place.* New York, NY: Farrar, Straus, and Giroux.

Klein, T. (2019, July 9). *Developing purposeful peak performers.* Retrieved from https://www
.gettingsmart.com/2019/07/developing-purposeful-peak-performers/

Knight, W. (2017, July 12). *Biased algorithms are everywhere, and no one seems to care.* Retrieved
from https://www.technologyreview.com/s/608248/biased-algorithms-are-everywhere-
and-no-one-seems-to-care/

Knowledge Works. (2017, January 12). *The future of learning: redefining readiness from the inside
out.* (2017, January 12). Retrieved from https://knowledgeworks.org/resources/future-
learning-redefining-readiness/.x

Kobie, N. (2019, June 7). *The complicated truth about China's social credit system.* Retrieved from
https://www.wired.co.uk/article/china-social-credit-system-explained

Korda, D. (2019, February 26). *What happens when we do school better?* Retrieved from https://
www.gettingsmart.com/2019/02/what-happens-when-we-do-school-better/

Lane-Zucker, L. (2016). *Place-based education, entrepreneurship and investing for an "impact Economy".*
Retrieved from https://www.linkedin.com/pulse/place-based-education-entrepreneurship-
investing-laurie-lane-Zucker/

Last year's wildfires were the most expensive in California history. (2019, May 8). Retrieved from
https://www.theguardian.com/us-news/2019/may/08/california-2018-wildfires-most-
expensive

Learning Outcomes. (n.d.). Retrieved from https://www.collegeunbound.org/apps/pages/skills

Leonhard, G. (2016). *Technology vs. humanity: The coming clash between man and machine.* FutureScapes.

Liebtag, E. (2016, December 24). *Rethinking high school: Badging, competency-based and real-world work.* Retrieved from https://www.gettingsmart.com/2016/10/rethinking-high-school-badging-competency-based-and-real-world-work/

Liebtag, E. (2017, April 24). *Santa Ana unified creating incredible pathways for students K–12.* Retrieved from https://www.gettingsmart.com/2017/04/santa-ana-unified-students-k–12/

Liebtag, E. (2017, May 31). *Transforming border learning experiences: New tech network in El Paso.* Retrieved from https://www.gettingsmart.com/2017/05/transforming-border-learning-experiences-new-tech-network-in-el-paso/

Liebtag, E. (2019, April 8). *Studio-based learning and self-directed students at NuVu.* Retrieved from https://www.gettingsmart.com/2019/04/studio-based-learning/

Liebtag, E. (2019, August 12). *Students use virtual reality to contribute to their communities.* Retrieved from https://www.gettingsmart.com/2019/08/students-use-virtual-reality-to-contribute-to-their-communities/

Liger Leadership Academy. (n.d.). Retrieved from http://www.ligeracademy.org/

Lippincott, J. (2019, December 11). *New guaranteed full-tuition scholarships and integrated work program.* Retrieved from https://antiochcollege.edu/2019/12/new-guaranteed-full-tuition-scholarships-and-integrated-work-program/

Lombardi, M. M. (2007, May). PDF.

Luks, A., & Payne, P. (2001). *The healing power of doing good: The health and spiritual benefits of helping others.* Bloomington, IN: iUniverse.com.

Manning, C. J. (2019, May 6). *Gen Z is the least religious generation. Here's why that could be a good thing.* Retrieved from https://psmag.com/ideas/gen-z-is-the-least-religious-generation-heres-why-that-could-be-a-good-thing

Matthews, D. (2019, May 22). *The radical plan to change how Harvard teaches economics.* Retrieved from https://www.vox.com/the-highlight/2019/5/14/18520783/harvard-economics-chetty

Michael Horn on choosing college. (2019, October 30). Getting Smart [Audio podcast]. Retrieved from https://www.gettingsmart.com/2019/10/podcast-michael-horn-on-choosing-college/

Midles, R. (2019, November 12). *Incubate, replicate and scale: How Dallas is creating great high school options.* Retrieved from https://www.gettingsmart.com/2019/11/incubate-replicate-and-scale-how-dallas-is-creating-great-high-school-options/

Miller, R. K. (2018). *Reimagining general education. Design thinking and intrinsic motivation perspectives.* Retrieved from https://www.aacu.org/sites/default/files/files/gened18/Plenary%20-%20Miller_0.pdf

Miller, R. K. (2018, February 15). *Reimagining general education: Design thinking and intrinsic motivation perspectives.* Retrieved from https://www.aacu.org/sites/default/files/files/gened18/Plenary - Miller_0.pdf

Minerva Schools at KGI. (2019). *The Development of CRISPR-dCas9 Activation gene editing technology as a form of hemophilia a treatment.* Retrieved from https://www.minerva.kgi.edu/academics/capstone-showcase-xiaotian-liao/

Mitra, D. (2006). Increasing student voice and moving toward youth leadership. *The Prevention Researcher, 13,* 7–10. Retrieved from https://eboardsecure.dcsdk12.org/attachments/080aee20-ba2b-4149-b28f-7d402eb4de1c.pdf

Moffitt, P. (n.d.). *Meaning of the Pali word "Dana."* Retrieved from http://dharmawisdom.org/teachings/articles/meaning-pali-word-dana

Mohr, K. (2018, September 17). *Teton Science Schools expands rural school network.* Retrieved from https://www.jhnewsandguide.com/the_hole_scroll/teton-science-schools-expands-rural-school-network/article_116ec362-fb50-511f-8fb6-d655caef09fa.html

Moody, H. R. (n.d.). *Baby boomers: From great expectations to a crisis of meaning.* Retrieved from https://www.asaging.org/blog/baby-boomers-great-expectations-crisis-meaning

Morningside College. (n.d.). *Project Siouxland.* Retrieved from https://www.morningside.edu/academics/project-siouxland/

Murayama, K. (2018). The science of motivation. *Psychological Science Agenda, 32*(6). Retrieved from https://www.apa.org/science/about/psa/2018/06/motivation

Murray, A., & Meyer, D. (2019, December 19). *What changes will the 2020s bring?* Retrieved from https://fortune.com/2019/12/19/2020s-predictions-ceo-daily/

National Academy of Engineering. (n.d.) *14 Grand Challenges for Engineering in the 21st Century.* Retrieved from http://www.engineeringchallenges.org/challenges.aspx

National Center for Education Statistics. (2019, May). *Undergraduate retention and graduation rates.* Retrieved from https://nces.ed.gov/programs/coe/indicator_ctr.asp

National Geographic. (n.d.) *Online Courses—Professional Learning Opportunities for Educators.* Retrieved from https://www.nationalgeographic.org/education/professional-development/courses/

NEA Foundation (n.d.). *Global Learning Fellowship—Field Study Experiences.* Retrieved from https://www.neafoundation.org/for-educators/global-learning-fellowship/

New Harmony High. (n.d.). Vision. Retrieved from https://newharmonyhigh.org/vision/

New Harmony High School. (n.d.). Retrieved from https://newharmonyhigh.org/

Niccolls, K. (2019, September 22). *Five learner-centered opportunities in Oakland.* Retrieved from https://www.gettingsmart.com/2019/09/five-learner-centered-opportunities-in-oakland/

Niehoff, M. (2020, January 12). *iLEAD Schools creating authentic, high quality project-based learning environments.* Retrieved from https://www.gettingsmart.com/2020/01/ilead-schools-creating-authentic-high-quality-project-based-learning-environments/

Noparstak, J. (n.d.). *Tikkun olam.* Retrieved from https://www.learningtogive.org/resources/tikkun-olam

Northeastern University. (2020). *Employer engagement and career design.* Retrieved from https://careers.northeastern.edu/experiential-learning/

Northeastern University. (n.d.) *Experiential learning.* Retrieved from https://careers.northeastern.edu/experiential-learning/

NPR. (2019, December 27). How colleges are using tech to keep track of students. *All Things Considered.* Retrieved from https://www.npr.org/2019/12/27/791918140/how-colleges-are-using-tech-to-keep-track-of-students

Nuthall, K., & Perez, B. (2018, August 2). *Reimagining high school in paramount USD.* Retrieved from https://www.gettingsmart.com/2018/08/reimagining-high-school-in-paramount-usd/

NuVu Studio. (2016, January 29). *Kate's story* [Video]. *YouTube.* Retrieved from https://www.youtube.com/watch? v=Eui55R3NerA&feature=emb_title

Olin College (n.d.). *Statement of founding precepts for Franklin W. Olin College of Engineering.* Retrieved from http://www.olin.edu/sites/default/files/olin_founding-precepts.pdf

Olin College of Engineering.(n.d.). *Curriculum.* Retrieved from http://www.olin.edu/academics/curriculum/

Oxfam. (2019). *Public good or private wealth*. Retrieved from https://oxfam.app.box .com/s/f9meuz1jrd9e1xrkrq59e37tpoppqup0/file/385579400762

Paul Quinn College. (n.d.). *Work Program*. Retrieved from http://www.pqc.edu/nation-building/work-program/

Pauli Murray Project. (n.d.). Retrieved from https://paulimurrayproject.org/pauli-murray/ faceup-mural-project/

Peck, M. S. (1998). *The different drum: Community making and peace*. New York, NY: Simon and Schuster.

Perelman School of Medicine, University of Pennsylvania. (n.d.). Faculty Affairs & Professional Development. Retrieved from https://www.med.upenn.edu/fapd/ assets/user-content/documents/AOMC%20Files/AOMC%20AcMed.Professionalism .Vol2.FINAL.pdf (p. 152)

Peters, A. (2019, February 14). *Most millennials would take a pay cut to work at a environmentally responsible company*. Retrieved from https://www.fastcompany.com/90306556/most-millennials-would-take-a-pay-cut-to-work-at-a-sustainable-company

Peters, M. A. (2019). *Encyclopedia of educational philosophy and theory*. Berlin, Germany: Springer.

Pitofsky, L. (2019, August 23). *Service learning: Designed to motivate and inspire*. Retrieved from https://www.gettingsmart.com/2019/08/service-learning-designed-to-motivate-and-inspire/

Possible Project. (n.d.). Retrieved from https://possibleproject.teamtailor.com/

Raymond, J. R., Sr., Maurana, C. A., & Kerschner, J. E. (2017). Expanding the health-care pipeline through innovation: The MCW model. *Transactions of the American Clinical and Climatological Association, 128*, 90–107. Retrieved from https://www.ncbi.nlm.nih.gov/ pmc/articles/PMC5525389/

Robinson, K. (2014). *Finding your element: How to discover your talents and passions and transform your life*. London, England: Penguin Books.

Rush University Medical Center. (n.d.). *The Health benefits of giving*. Retrieved from https:// www.rush.edu/health-wellness/discover-health/health-benefits-giving

Russell, S. (2019). *Human compatible: Artificial intelligence and the problem of control*. New York, NY: Viking.

Rusu, A. S. (2019). *Interdisciplinary learning objective for service-learning curricula: Neurobiological and evolutionary explanations of helping others*. Palma, Spain: EDULEARN19 Proceedings. Retrieved from https://doi.org/10.21125/edulearn.2019.0571.

Samarrai, F. (2020). Computer science students build coronavirus tracking website. *UVA Today. University of Virginia*. Retrieved from https://news.virginia.edu/content/computer-science-students-build-coronavirus-tracking-website?utm_source=ULinkedIn&utm_ medium=social&utm_campaign=news

Schawbel, D. (2014, March 11). *Seth Godin: The future of education and the current state of marketing*. Retrieved from https://www.forbes.com/sites/danschawbel/2014/03/11/seth -godin-the-future-of-education-and-the-current-state-of-marketing/#15f925691161

School Network. (n.d.). Retrieved from https://www.tetonscience.org/what-we-do/school-network/

Schreier, H. M. C., Schonert-Reichl, K. A., & Chen, E. (2013). Effect of volunteering on risk factors for cardiovascular disease in adolescents. *JAMA Pediatrics, 167*(4), 327. Retrieved from https://doi.org/10.1001/jamapediatrics.2013.1100.

Schwartz, M. S. (2019, December 28). *Virginia school district to give students one day off per year for "civic engagement."* Retrieved from https://www.npr.org/2019/12/27/791889392/fairfax-va-schools-to-give-students-one-day-off-per-year-for-civic-engagement?fbclid=IwAR1Y67Jzv1xobMEVf6yy4VKdjmeta5Rpu-13vqqqZ77K-RzgdHyT26m_INk

Service learning micro-credentials. (n.d.). Retrieved from https://microcredentials.digitalpromise.org/explore? tag=Service Learning

Service learning. (n.d.). Retrieved from https://aglobalteacher.weebly.com/service-learning.html

Share the World's Resources. (2010, November 17). *The wisdom of indigenous cultures.* Retrieved from https://www.sharing.org/information-centre/articles/wisdom-indigenous-cultures

Siouxland News (2019). *Morningside College, Western Iowa Tech team up for Project Siouxland.* Retrieved from https://siouxlandnews.com/news/local/morningside-college-western-iowa-tech-team-up-for-project-siouxland

Smith, G. A. (2012). Can schools help create a post-capitalist world? *ENCOUNTER: Education for Meaning and Social Justice, 25*(2), 2–14. Retrieved from http://boggscenter.org/wp-content/uploads/2012/09/Smith253-3.pdf

Societal Reform Corporation. (n.d.). Service Hours. (n.d.). Retrieved from https://societalreform.org/service-hours

South, J. (2018, December 27). MIA in school: Instilling a sense of purpose in students. *EdSurge News.* Retrieved from https://www.edsurge.com/news/2017-10-27-mia-in-school-instilling-a-sense-of-purpose-in-students

Southeast Michigan Stewardship Coalition. (n.d.). Retrieved from https://semiscoalition.org/

Stafford-Brizard, K. B., & Cantor, P. (2016). *Building blocks for learning: A framework for comprehensive student development.* Retrieved from https://turnaroundusa.org/wp-content/uploads/2016/03/Turnaround-for-Children-Building-Blocks-for-Learningx-2.pdf

Statista. (2019). *Number of internet of things (IoT) connected devices worldwide in 2018, 2025 and 2030.* Retrieved from https://www.statista.com/statistics/802690/worldwide-connected-devices-by-access-technology/

Stefon, M. (2010). *Islamic beliefs and practices.* New York, NY: Britannica Educational, published in association with Rosen Educational Services.

Steinauer-Scudder, C. (n.d.). *The seeds of ancestors: A day at soul fire farm.* Retrieved from https://emergencemagazine.org/story/the-seeds-of-ancestors/

Strikwerda, C. J. (2018, January 28). *Why community colleges are good for you.* Retrieved from https://www.chronicle.com/article/Why-Community-Colleges-Are/242359

Support the *Guardian.* (2019). *Last year's wildfires were the most expensive in California history.* Retrieved from https://www.theguardian.com/us-news/2019/may/08/california-2018-wildfires-most-expensive

TaishiConsulting10. (2012, April 4). *Peter Senge on the Future of Education* [Video]. *YouTube.* Retrieved from https://www.youtube.com/watch? v=BakP-DaRRHI&feature =youtube

Take Action Global (n.d.). About Us. Retrieved from http://takeactionglobal.org/about.html

Teach SDGs. (n.d.). About. Retrieved from http://www.teachsdgs.org/about.html

Teaching through the SDGs. (n.d.). Retrieved from https://aglobalteacher.weebly.com/teachsdgs.html

TeachSDGs. (n.d.). About. Retrieved from http://www.teachsdgs.org/about.html

Thornburg, D. (2013). *From the campfire to the holodeck: Creating engaging and powerful 21st century learning environments*. Jossey-Bass.

Thurston Talk. (2019, September 9) Washington Monthly *names Evergreen "Best in Nation" in master's university category*. Retrieved September 11, 2019, from https://www.thurstontalk.com/2019/09/09/washington-monthly-names-evergreen-best-in-nation-in-masters-university-category/

Toms, M., & Toms, J. W. (1999). *True work: Doing what you love and loving what you do*. Bell Tower.

Turney, C. S. M., Palmer, J., Maslin, M., Hogg, A., Fogwill, C. J., Southon, J., . . . Hua, Q. (2018). Global peak in atmospheric radiocarbon provides a potential definition for the onset of the anthropocene epoch in 1965. *Scientific Reports, 8*, 3293. Retrieved from https://doi.org/10.1038/s41598-018-20970-5.

U.S. News. (n.d.) Evergreen State College Overall Rankings | US News Best Colleges. Retrieved from https://www.usnews.com/best-colleges/evergreen-state-college-8155/overall-rankings

University of North Carolina–Asheville. (n.d.). *Greenfest*. Retrieved from https://sustainability.unca.edu/greenfest

Using artificial intelligence to solve problems in communities. (2019). *Getting Smart* [Audio podcast]. Retrieved from https://www.gettingsmart.com/2019/05/podcast-using-artificial-intelligence-to-solve-problems-in-communities/

ValuePenguin. (2019). *Average student loan debt in America: 2019 facts and figures. Retrieved from https://www.valuepenguin.com/average-student-loan-debt*

Vandeborne, L., & Fujii, S. (2016). *Community conversations shape portrait of a graduate*. Retrieved from https://www.gettingsmart.com/2016/01/community-conversations-shape-portrait-graduate/

Vander Ark, C. (2019, January 13). *Learning gardens provide equity, access and great food*. Retrieved from https://www.gettingsmart.com/2019/01/learning-gardens-provide-equity-access-and-great-food/

Vander Ark, T. (2016, December 24). *El Paso ISD adopts active learning with plan that powers innovation*. Retrieved from https://www.gettingsmart.com/2016/03/el-paso-adopts-active-learning-with-plan-that-powers-innovation/

Vander Ark, T. (2016, July 19). *Dual language education for equity & economic development*. Retrieved from https://www.gettingsmart.com/2016/07/dual-language-education-for-equity-economic-development/

Vander Ark, T. (2017, January 24). Google's Jaime Casap on inequity and inquiry [Audio podcast]. Getting Smart. Retrieved from https://www.gettingsmart.com/2017/01/getting-smart-podcast-googles-jaime-casap-on-inequity-and-inquiry/

Vander Ark, T. (2018, April 24). *Community defined projects at health leadership high*. Retrieved from https://www.gettingsmart.com/2018/04/community-defined-projects-at-health-leadership-high/

Vander Ark, T. (2018, August 28). *20 ways blockchain will transform (OK, may improve) education*. Retrieved from https://www.gettingsmart.com/2018/08/20-ways-blockchain-will-transform-ok-may-improve-education/

Vander Ark, T. (2018, January 12). *Ask about AI: The future of learning and work*. Retrieved from https://www.gettingsmart.com/2017/11/ask-about-ai-the-future-of-learning-and-work/

Vander Ark, T. (2018, July 17). *Asking kids to dream—and bringing dreams to life*. Retrieved from https://www.gettingsmart.com/2018/07/asking-kids-to-dream-and-bringing-dreams-to-life

Vander Ark, T. (2018, November 12). *The coming social economy*. Retrieved from https://www.gettingsmart.com/2018/11/the-coming-social-economy/

Vander Ark, T. (2018, October 8). *Curbing killer robots and other misuses of AI*. Retrieved from https://www.gettingsmart.com/2018/10/curbing-killer-robots-and-other-misuses-of-ai/

Vander Ark, T. (2019, February 25). How to Be Employable Forever. Retrieved from https://www.gettingsmart.com/2019/02/how-to-be-employable-forever/

Vander Ark, T. (2019, April 1). *The promise and implications of artificial intelligence in education*. Retrieved from https://www.gettingsmart.com/2019/04/smart-review-the-promise-and-implications-of-artificial-intelligence-in-education/

Vander Ark, T. (2019, April 11). *Contribution: Schools alive with possibility*. Retrieved from https://www.gettingsmart.com/2019/04/contribution-schools-alive-with-possibility

Vander Ark, T. (2019, April 22). *College Unbound helps working adults earn fast affordable degrees*. Retrieved from https://www.forbes.com/sites/tomvanderark/2019/04/22/college-unbound-helps-working-adults-earn-fast-affordable-degrees/#5e5fe78c7a93

Vander Ark, T. (2019, August 26). *Acton academy: Hero launch pad goes global*. Retrieved from https://www.gettingsmart.com/2019/08/acton-academy-hero-launch-pad-goes-global/

Vander Ark, T. (2019, December 16). *Your work is to discover your work: On calling and contribution*. Retrieved from https://www.forbes.com/sites/tomvanderark/2019/12/16/your-work-is-to-discover-your-work-on-calling-and-contribution/#69e0f5e33dce

Vander Ark, T. (2019, December 20). *Early college: The little reform bundle that could*. Retrieved from https://www.gettingsmart.com/2019/12/early-college-the-little-reform-bundle-that-could/

Vander Ark, T. (2019, January 15). *Why every high school should require an AI course*. Retrieved from https://www.gettingsmart.com/2019/01/why-every-high-school-should-require-an-ai-course/

Vander Ark, T. (2019, June 17). *10 signs of progress in engineering for the earth, energy and environment*. Retrieved from https://www.gettingsmart.com/2019/06/10-signs-of-progress-in-engineering-for-the-earth-energy-and-environment/

Vander Ark, T. (2019, March 15). *Organizing your school as a list of courses doesn't work for learners*. Retrieved from https://www.gettingsmart.com/2019/03/organizing-your-school-as-a-list-of-courses-doesnt-work-for-learners/

Vander Ark, T. (2019, March 20). *Blending engineering, entrepreneurial mindset, and an appreciation for the variety of the human condition*. Retrieved from https://www.gettingsmart.com/2019/03/blending-engineering-entrepreneurial-mindset-and-an-appreciation-for-the-variety-of-the-human-condition/

Vander Ark, T. (2019, May 29). *Engineering good in the world*. Retrieved from https://www.gettingsmart.com/2019/05/engineering-good-in-the-world/

Vander Ark, T. (2019, May 29). *Purdue poly: Driven by equity, solving community challenges*. Retrieved from https://www.gettingsmart.com/2019/05/purdue-poly-driven-by-equity-solving-community-challenges/

Vander Ark, T. (2019, May 5). *The coming social economy*. Retrieved from https://www .gettingsmart.com/2018/11/the-coming-social-economy/

Vander Ark, T. (2019, October 21). *Learning to make a difference at One Stone*. Retrieved from https://www.gettingsmart.com/2019/10/learning-to-make-a-difference-at-one-stone/

Vander Ark, T. (2019, September 10). *Why schools need signature learning experiences*. Retrieved from https://www.gettingsmart.com/2019/09/why-schools-need-signature-learning-experiences/

Vander Ark, T. (2020, January 17). *Why your community needs an environmental sustainability coordinator.* Retrieved from https://www.forbes.com/sites/tomvanderark/2020/01/17/why-your-community-needs-an-environmental-sustainability-coordinator/#6ff622213d38

Vander Ark, T. (2020, January 6). *24 goals to save the planet (in case we don't)*. Retrieved from https://www.forbes.com/sites/tomvanderark/2020/01/06/24-goals-to-save-the-planet-1-in-case-we-dont

Vander Ark, T., & Liebtag, E. (2018, February 13). *Collaboration: Key to successful teams and projects*. (2018). Retrieved from https://www.gettingsmart.com/2018/02/collaboration-key-to-successful-teams-and-projects/

Veith, G. E. (2016, March 30). *Martin Luther on vocation and serving our neighbors*. Retrieved from https://acton.org/pub/commentary/2016/03/30/martin-luther-vocation-and-serving -our-neighbors

Viscott, D. (1993). Retrieved from https://www.goodreads.com/quotes/7407260-the-purpose-of-life-is-to-discover-your-gift-the

Vox. (2019) The radical plan to change how Harvard teaches economics. Retrieved from https://www.vox.com/the-highlight/2019/5/14/18520783/harvard-economics-chetty

Walton, J. (2018, February 27). *Global Dignity launch materials to encourage development of dignity*. Retrieved from https://www.gettingsmart.com/2018/02/global-dignity-launch-materials-to-encourage-development-of-dignity/

Walton, J. (2018, October 15). *Global Dignity Day: Teaching compassion, understanding and tolerance*. Retrieved from https://www.gettingsmart.com/2018/10/global-dignity-day-teaching-compassion-understanding-and-tolerance/

Wilson, T. (2018, January 31). *Martin Luther King Jr: "It really boils down to this: That all life is interrelated," Interconnected World sermon*. Retrieved from https://speakola.com/ideas/martin-luther-king-jr-interconnected-world-massey-5-1967

Wojcicki, E. (2019). Esther Wojcicki on raising successful people [Audio podcast]. Getting Smart. Retrieved from https://www.gettingsmart.com/2019/07/podcast-esther-wojcicki-on-raising-successful-people/

Wong, A. (2019, January 23). *America's teachers are furious*. Retrieved from https://www.theatlantic.com/education/archive/2019/01/teachers-are-launching-a-rebellion/580975/

Wood, M. (2019, April 29). *What else can Big Data do? Pick stocks*. Retrieved from https://www .marketplace.org/2018/09/20/tech/big-data-do-pick-stock/

XQ Institute. (2019, December 9). *Computer science through a lens of equity & social justice*. Retrieved from https://xqsuperschool.org/blog/student-success/computer-science-equity-social-justice/

XQ Institute. (2019a). *This is Latitude 37.8 High School.* Retrieved from https://xqsuperschool.org/xq-schools/latitude-high-school

XQ Institute. (2019b). *This is New Harmony.* Retrieved from https://xqsuperschool.org/xq-schools/new-harmony

XQ Institute. (2020). *Students share what it's like to learn in an Innovative High School.* Retrieved from https://xqsuperschool.org/blog/student-voice/students-innovative-high-school/

YouthBuild Stories. (n.d.). *YouthBuild.* Retrieved from https://www.youthbuild.org/stories

YouthBuild. (n.d.). Retrieved from https://www.youthbuild.org/

INDEX

Leadership That Makes an Impact

MICHAEL FULLAN & MARY JEAN GALLAGHER

With the goal of transforming the culture of learning to develop greater equity, excellence, and student well-being, this book will help you liberate the system and maintain focus.

PETER M. DEWITT

This step-by-step how-to guide presents the six driving forces of instructional leadership within a multistage model for implementation, delivering lasting improvement through small collaborative changes.

BRYAN GOODWIN

If you've ever wondered anything, really—just out of curiosity—then you have what it takes to lead your school to restored curiosity and your students to well-being and success.

JOHN HATTIE & RAYMOND L. SMITH

Based on the most current Visible Learning® research with contributions from education thought leaders around the world, this book includes practical ideas for leaders to implement high-impact strategies to strengthen entire school cultures and advocate for all students.

DAVIS CAMPBELL & MICHAEL FULLAN

The model outlined in this book develops a systems approach to governing local schools collaboratively to become exemplars of highly effective decision-making, leadership, and action.

MICHAEL FULLAN, JOANNE QUINN, & JOANNE MCEACHEN

The comprehensive strategy of deep learning incorporates practical tools and processes to engage educational stakeholders in new partnerships, mobilize whole-system change, and transform learning for all students.

JOANNE QUINN, JOANNE MCEACHEN, MICHAEL FULLAN, MAG GARDNER, & MAX DRUMMY

Dive into deep learning with this hands-on guide to creating learning experiences that give purpose, unleash student potential, and transform not only learning, but life itself.

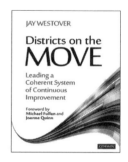

JAY WESTOVER

The transformative framework outlined in this book creates a districtwide approach for changing the culture of learning and creating a coherent system of continuous improvement.

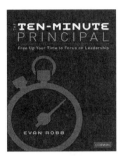

ANTHONY KIM, KEARA MASCARENAZ, & KAWAI LAI

This guide provides battle-tested practices to help leaders build better habits for team learning, meetings, and projects, to achieve a more responsive, innovative organization.

EVAN ROBB

Build the foundations of effective leadership despite daily distractions. Learn how to intentionally use ten-minute opportunities to consider and execute your vision.

AMY TEPPER & PATRICK FLYNN

Nineteen strategies help leaders, coaches, and teachers improve their ability to identify desired outcomes, recognize learning in action, collect relevant evidence, and develop effective feedback.

JULIE M. WILSON

Learn to make sense of challenging change journeys and accelerate implementation with this practical framework that includes human-centered tools, resources, and mini case studies.

GRANT LICHTMAN

Our rapidly evolving world is dramatically impacting how we view schools. *Thrive* shows educators how they can help their schools not only survive but thrive during rapid change.

ERIC SHENINGER

The future-forward framework in this book prepares leaders to harness the power of innovative ideas and digital strategies to create relevant, engaging, and intuitive school cultures.

CHRISTINE MASON, PAUL LIABENOW, & MELISSA PATSCHKE

Envision and enact transformative change with an iterative visioning process, thought-provoking vignettes, case studies from exemplary schools, key strategies and tools, and practical implementation ideas.

KIRSTEN RICHERT, JEFFREY IKLER, & MARGARET ZACCHEI

Shifting empowers educational change leaders to proactively and coherently navigate complex, unprecedented change in schools and establish a school culture in which changemakers can thrive.

CORWIN

A SAGE Publishing Company

Helping educators make the greatest impact

CORWIN HAS ONE MISSION: to enhance education through intentional professional learning.

We build long-term relationships with our authors, educators, clients, and associations who partner with us to develop and continuously improve the best evidence-based practices that establish and support lifelong learning.